Enhancing Women's Participation in Economic Development

A World Bank Policy Paper

The World Bank
Washington, D.C.

Library of Congress Cataloging-in-Publication Data

Enhancing women's participation in economic development.
     p. cm. — (A World Bank policy paper)
  Includes bibliographical references.
  ISBN 0-8213-2963-4
  1. Women in development. 2. Women—Education. 3. Women—
Employment.   I. International Bank for Reconstruction and
Development.   II. Series.
HQ1240.E37   1994
331.4—dc20   94-26311
                                             CIP

Cover design by Walton Rosenquist and Beni Chibber-Rao

ISSN 1014-8124

Contents

3

Boxes

Tables

Figures

Acknowledgments

This paper was written by K. Subbarao in collaboration with Jyotsna Jalan, Kathleen Newland, and Carolyn Winter. The work was carried out under the direction of Minh Chau Nguyen and the overall guidance of K. Y. Amoako. This paper draws on extensive analytical work done both within and outside the bank and was especially aided by the initial guidance of Barbara Herz and by background papers written by Kowsar Choudhury, Sharon Holt, Jyotsna Jalan, Elizabeth Katz, Agnes Quisumbing, Elizabeth Rhyne, and Guilherme Sedlacek. Extensive comments and suggestions were provided by World Bank staff in the regions, in the central vice-presidencies, and in the Operations Evaluation Department. Bruce Ross-Larson provided editorial advice. Benjamin Crow produced drafts of the paper.

Foreword

Enhancing women's participation in development is essential not only for achieving social justice but also for reducing poverty. Worldwide experience shows clearly that supporting a stronger role for women contributes to economic growth, it improves child survival and overall family health, and it reduces fertility, thus helping to slow population growth rates. In short, investing in women is central to sustainable development.

And yet, despite these known returns, women still face many barriers in contributing to and benefiting from development. The barriers begin with comparatively low investment in female education and health, they continue with restricted access to services and assets, and they are made worse by legal and regulatory constraints on women's opportunities. As a result, the worldwide progress in development over the last three decades has not translated into proportional gains for women.

This paper points to actions that can help to turn around this inequitable situation. Evidence of what works is particularly strong in five areas: education, health, wage labor, agriculture and natural resource management, and financial services. The paper also suggests a broadening of the "women in development" approach toward a "gender and development" strategy that takes into account the relative roles and responsibilities of women *and* men and recognizes that, to effect long-term change in the conditions of women, the actions and attitudes of men must change.

The World Bank is committed to mainstreaming gender concerns into its operations, and significant steps have already been taken in this direction. There remains, however, a long way to go. Moreover, the Bank is only one of the many actors engaged in trying to close the gender gap. We continue to collaborate with and learn from our partners—governments, other international institutions, and nongovernmental organizations—in our joint effort to meet the goal of ensuring women's full participation in development.

Lewis T. Preston
President
The World Bank

Executive Summary

Women produce half the food in some parts of the developing world, bear most of the responsibility for household food security, and make up a quarter of the work force in industry and a third in services. In addition to income-generating activities (in cash and kind), women's household activities include caring for the sick, house maintenance, and such vital work as caring for children, preparing food, and fetching firewood and water. Yet, because of women's more limited access to education and other opportunities, their productivity relative to their potential remains low. Improving women's productivity can contribute to growth, efficiency, and poverty reduction—key development goals everywhere.

Investing proportionally more in women than in men—in education, health, family planning, access to land, inputs, and extension—is, thus, an important part of development strategy, as well as an act of social justice. It directly reduces poverty through substantial economic and social payoffs. It leads to higher productivity and more efficient use of resources. It contributes to environmentally sustainable development. It produces significant social gains—lower fertility, better household nutrition, and reduced infant, child, and maternal mortality. The intergenerational gains are particularly striking: the mother's education has a stronger impact on the health and education of her children than does the father's. Studies also show that income controlled by women is more likely to be spent on household needs than income controlled by men.

Gaps and Barriers

The payoffs notwithstanding, the gender gap remains substantial in many countries. Girls' school enrollment rates lag behind those of boys.

Women are channeled into disciplines with low payoffs. In many countries, dropout rates are higher for girls than for boys. In a few countries in South Asia and Africa, discrimination in food intake and health care means that women's natural health advantage at birth is quickly eroded, if not reversed, resulting in lower life expectancies for women than men. Pregnancy and childbirth remain major causes of women's mortality.

The worldwide progress in social and economic development over the past three decades has not translated into proportional gains for women. The reasons: limited options and formidable barriers. The barriers include low investment in women's education and health, poor access to services and assets, and legal and regulatory barriers that restrict women's options. Many more women than men are in low-paying, low-skilled informal activities, but those in the formal labor force fare no better: occupational segregation channels them into less productive and less remunerative segments of the labor market.

Parents in developing countries are less likely to send their daughters to school than their sons: the direct and indirect costs of education are higher for girls than for boys, and the benefits to parents are remote and uncertain. Lower educational attainment, in turn, places women at a disadvantage in the labor market, perpetuating the cycle of low earnings and low investment in education. For similar reasons, families spend less on health care for girls.

Women in developing countries lack access to family planning services. The combination of poor education and poor access to services can be deadly—as prevailing high maternal mortality rates testify.

In spite of women's significant role in managing household water and sanitation, a variety of barriers, often relating to location, design, staffing, and scheduling issues, reduce women's access to services. For example, the siting of facilities may not recognize gender differences that affect mobility around the village.

Women who brave the odds to operate as farm managers and agricultural workers rarely benefit from extension services. Few extension agents are women, and overloaded extension systems tend to concentrate on men's crops and activities. There are also barriers that prevent women from playing their role in the conservation of natural resources. Social and institutional factors such as lack of access to land and information often undermine women's ability to maintain environmental quality and sustainable use of resources.

Lack of access to credit for female entrepreneurs limits the profitability and growth of their enterprises. Limited education and mobility—and, in some cases, cultural barriers—restrict women's contact with institutions that offer financial services, as do the high transaction costs and collateral requirements associated with making small loans.

Legal and regulatory barriers that do not apply to men exacerbate the inefficiencies of inequity. Property, especially land—the universal collateral—is usually registered in a man's name. Some countries have laws that prevent women from entering into contracts in their own names or from owning or selling land. In other countries, legal and regulatory restrictions prevent women from participating in the labor force on equal terms with men.

The need to balance home and market responsibilities is a major constraint on women's earnings, productivity, and accumulation of human capital. The lack of affordable childcare forces women into jobs with flexible hours and locations but the consequences are often lower earnings, discontinuities in work, limited mobility, and lower levels of skill.

Reducing the Barriers

Several effective strategies for reducing the barriers to women's economic participation have emerged from the past two decades of project experience. It should be stressed that the experience gained so far is inevitably country specific. However, there is particularly strong evidence of what works in five areas: education, health, wage labor, agriculture and natural resource management, and financial services.

Education. Strategies for expanding girls' enrollment include reserving places for girls, establishing single-sex schools or classrooms, recruiting more female teachers, and designing school facilities to conform to the cultural standards of the community. In some countries, it may also be necessary to reduce the direct and indirect costs of education to persuade parents to send their daughters to school as well as their sons. Scholarships for girls, flexible hours to allow girls to complete home chores before or after school, and provision of childcare for younger siblings have proved successful in raising girls' attendance. Projects that improve home technologies and reduce the time required to provide the household with water or fuel have also freed time for girls to go to school.

Health. Community-based health services have been cost-effective in improving women's health. Integrated services—which combine nutrition, family planning, maternal and child health services, and primary health care—tend to be the most effective in reaching women. Certain interventions have proven particularly cost-effective, including iron and iodine supplementation, calorie supplementation for pregnant women, family planning, and, where it is legal, safe ending of unwanted pregnancy. In some settings, the availability of women as health providers is especially important.

Wage labor. The principal strategies for increasing women's participation in the formal labor force include removing legal and regulatory barriers, raising women's productivity, easing the constraints on their time, and improving the efficiency of the labor market by providing information on job opportunities. Legal reform, education and training, improved access to information, and affordable childcare are the keys for enhancing women's participation in formal labor markets.

Agriculture and natural resource management. Because most poor rural women work in agriculture, the main strategy is to help women obtain title to the land they farm and to open the door to services and government assistance. Women also should be enabled to exercise the full range of land rights—to sell or mortgage the land—and to get the full benefit from crop sales.

Environmental degradation increases women's burden, as they have to trek long distances to fetch fuelwood and water. The direct and indirect costs of environmental damage for women need to be assessed and included in natural resource management projects and policies. Women's participation in decisions on issues relating to environmental policies is critical for setting appropriate priorities. Women can participate more effectively if they are trained in the analysis of the causes and consequences of environmental problems.

Financial services. Innovative programs have demonstrated that financial services, mainly credit and savings, can be provided to poor women at competitive cost. Group lending has broken down the barriers of high transaction costs, high perceived risks of default, and lack of collateral. Institutions that have experimented with such innovative strategies—such as the Grameen Bank in Bangladesh—have much higher repayment rates than national commercial banking systems.

The World Bank's Strategy

The World Bank's early "women in development" programs tended to treat women as a special target group of beneficiaries in projects and programs. The policy framework is now broadening to reflect the ways in which the relations between women and men constrain or advance efforts to boost growth and reduce poverty for all. This focus characterizes the "gender and development" approach—which the Bank will promote to enhance women's contributions to development. The Bank's future analytical work will focus on gender differentiation and the factors underlying the structure of gender relations within households.

The Bank will support member governments in designing and implementing promising policies and programs, concentrating on the areas where accumulated experience provides clear and unambiguous operational direction. Effective program delivery depends on careful design, monitoring, evaluation, and staff training—areas in which the Bank has now gained some experience. The Bank can also help governments mobilize external donors' resources to address gender disparities.

The Bank is committed to integrating gender issues into the mainstream of its own approach, including focusing on countries and areas where underinvestment in women has been acute. Gender issues will be systematically addressed in country assistance strategies—and in the design and implementation of lending programs, including adjustment operations. The Bank's policy-oriented analytical work will continue to advance the conceptual and operational knowledge of the gender and development approach.

Successful implementation of this strategy will require intensified staff training, some shift in the mix of skills available, and some degree of resource reallocation within country departments—and possibly, across departments or regions. Bank staff need to be sensitized to the importance of integrating gender issues into Bank operations. There is also a need for dissemination of analytical work, operational tools, and good practices to staff and member countries. Carrying out analytical work, pilot programs, and impact evaluations may imply a need for specialized staff skills that may not be adequately available at present. Finally, particularly in countries where acute gender disparities exist, it is likely that operationalization of the strategy will imply significant reallocations of resources within country departments.

The Bank is only one of the contributors to the international effort to advance women's status and participation in economic development. Other donors and international institutions play important roles in closing the gender gap. The Bank will continue to learn from and collaborate with other agencies and to capitalize on existing expertise that exists in advancing gender issues on the development agenda. All these efforts, however, will be fruitful only with governments' leadership, commitment, and collaboration.

1

An Overview

There are, it is true, considerable numbers of matters where practical action is delayed by the absence of sufficient knowledge. There are more perhaps where our knowledge is sufficient to occupy us for the next twenty years, and where the continuance of social evils is not due to the fact that we do not know what is right, but to the fact that we prefer to continue doing what is wrong. Those who have the power to remove them have not the will, and those who have the will have not, as yet, the power.

C. Tawney
(as quoted in Harriss, Guhan, and Cassen 1992)

Women make up 40 percent of the world's work force in agriculture, a quarter in industry, and a third in services. Women farmers in the developing countries grow at least 50 percent of the world's food—as much as 80 percent in some African countries. In addition to income-generating activities (in cash and kind), women's household activities include caring for the sick, house maintenance, and such vital work as caring for children, preparing food, and fetching firewood and water. Yet, women's productivity remains low—both in income-generating work and in home production. Improving women's productivity can contribute to growth, efficiency, and poverty reduction—key development goals everywhere.

Investing in women—in education, health, family planning, access to land, inputs, and extension—is thus an important part of development strategy as well as a matter of social justice. It is an integral part of the Bank's overall strategy for poverty reduction that calls for broadly based, labor-absorbing economic growth and improved human resource development.

If long-term change in the conditions of women is to be achieved, the actions and attitudes of men must change, and it is important that men be brought along in the process of change. For example, family planning information campaigns should be aimed at men as well as at women because it is when men and women are able to make joint informed decisions on family size, child spacing, and appropriate methods of contraception, that these programs are most successful. Likewise, problems affecting women are often closely related to the social relationships between men and women. For example, many women's health problems are embedded in unequal gender relations in work loads, responsibilities for family welfare, and access to resources and decisionmaking, it is impossible to deal effectively with women's health problems through approaches that deal only with women.

The lessons from strategies and projects now extend the women in development approach to an even broader field. Development organizations have begun to recognize that the best way to ensure that women are not left at the margin of the development process is to analyze the relative roles and responsibilities of men and women and to apply the insights gained from this research to the design of programs and projects. This, in essence, constitutes the gender and development approach.

Far from being antithetical to the women in development approach, the gender and development approach builds on what has been achieved so far. Because in almost all cases the disparities handicap women rather than men, the gender and development approach—like its predecessor—is aimed at achieving complementary goals for men and women. The emphasis is on gender relations in the family and in the community rather than on women in isolation.

The gender and development approach distinguishes between practical and strategic needs of women. Practical needs refer to the demand for goods and services arising out of women's socially acceptable roles in society—such as the need for health care or drinking water supplies. Strategic needs refer to requirements, such as equal employment opportunities and equal access to education and to productive assets, that would help women achieve greater equality relative to men by changing their position in society. Interventions that are aimed at meeting practical needs seldom arouse controversy or hostile reactions as they do not alter the subordinate position of women in the society. By contrast, interventions to meet strategic needs can be controversial because they challenge women's subordinate status in the society.[1]

In addressing the needs of women, a donor organization such as the World Bank must be sensitive to the prevailing social and cultural factors in its member countries. This can best be done by focusing on strong economic arguments showing that women can and must play a full role in the economic development of their countries. This strategy will not only contribute to raising women's social status and eventually equalizing it with that of men but also be an asset for the countries' economic development.

Gender Gaps in Education

Across the world, significant improvements have been made in women's education, health, and access to labor market opportunities. However, compared with men, women remain at a disadvantage in nearly all socioeconomic spheres.

Both boys and girls have benefited from enormous expansion in school enrollments at all levels of education, but girls still lag behind. In the developing countries in 1960, there were 67 females per 100 males enrolled in primary school; in 1990, there were 86 females per 100 males. Trends are similar for secondary and tertiary enrollments (Figure 1): 53 females per 100 males in secondary schools in 1960 and 75 in 1990; and 36 females per 100 males in tertiary education in 1960 compared with 64 by

Figure 1.   School Enrollment for Females Still Lags Behind That for Males in Developing Countries

Females per 100 males

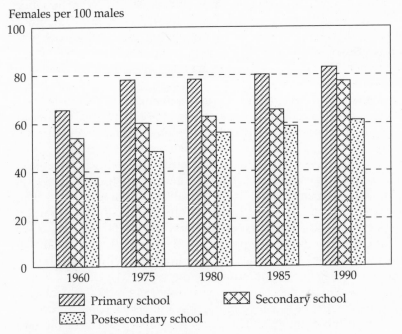

Source: UNESCO Statistical Yearbook 1991.

Table 1. School Enrollments Are More Equal in Transitional Economies

Country	Primary		Secondary	
	1970	*1990*	*1970*	*1990*
Bulgaria	94	93	—	98
Czech Republic	96	97	183	132
Hungary	99	99	102	137
Poland	93	95	—	—
Romania	97	106	151	174

—. Not available.

Note: The numbers refer primarily to general secondary education and do not include students (mostly males) enrolled in technical and vocational schools or full-time apprenticeships.

Source: World Bank 1993a.

1990. However, in the transitional economies, even as early as 1970, there was near gender parity in both primary and secondary school enrollments, and girls' educational qualifications when leaving school often exceeded those of boys (Table 1).

In postsecondary institutions, as Figure 2 shows, women continue to be overrepresented relative to men in some fields of study: teacher training, the humanities, theology, fine and applied arts, home economics, and

Figure 2. Gender Streaming Excludes Many Women from Male-Dominated Fields

Females per 100 students by field of study

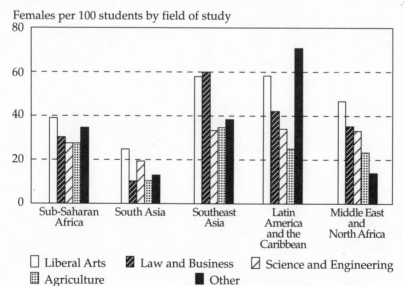

Source: United Nations Statistical Office 1990; World Bank staff estimates.

service trades. "Gender streaming" arises because in many countries women acquire skills at the primary and secondary school levels that prepare them only for predominantly feminized professions such as teaching. Such gender streaming prevents women from getting training in applied scientific fields such as agriculture, forestry, fishing, science, and engineering. Gender streaming is to be found even in Eastern Europe (Czech and Slovak Republics, Hungary, and Poland) and, to some extent, Russia.

Gender Gaps in Health

Over the past two decades, life expectancy at birth has risen for men and women in all regions of the world. In South Asia and Sub-Saharan Africa, female life expectancy is less than 60 years, compared with 71 years in Latin America and the Caribbean. In the transitional economies of Europe and Central Asia, the trends in the average life expectancies of men and women show a pattern similar to that observed in the industrial countries, where the average life expectancy for women is five to eight years longer than for men. But in some South Asian countries— Bangladesh, Bhutan, India, Nepal, and Pakistan—men either outlive or have the same life expectancy as women, notwithstanding the biological advantages females enjoy (Table 2).

Among all the causes of death for women, maternal mortality continues to be the most significant. About 500,000 women die each year from the direct complications of pregnancy and childbirth. In developing countries, on average, the maternal mortality ratio is 290 deaths per 100,000 births, compared with 24 in industrial nations (Table 3). Countries in South Asia have among the highest ratios, with some countries having more than 1,500 maternal deaths per 100,000 live births.

Table 2. In Some Countries, Females Die at an Earlier Age Than Males

Country or region	Female	Male
Bangladesh	52	53
India	60	60
Nepal	53	54
Pakistan	59	59
East Asia and the Pacific	66	66
Europe and Central Asia	74	66
High-income economies	80	73
Middle East and North Africa	65	63
South Asia	59	59
Sub-Saharan Africa	52	49

Source: World Bank 1993a, Table 32.

Table 3.   Childbirth Is Still a Major Cause of Mortality in Many Developing Countries
(maternal mortality per 100,000 births)

Bhutan	1,710
Ghana	1,000
Nigeria	800
Bangladesh	600
Senegal	600
Pakistan	500
Indonesia	450
Paraguay	365
Colombia	126
Russian Federation	49
Average developing countries	290
Average industrial countries	24

Source: United Nations Statistical Office 1990.

Gender Gaps in Employment

Between 1970 and 1985 the percentage of economically active women declined in Sub-Saharan Africa and in South Asia (Figure 3). This finding needs to be interpreted with caution because in some countries women's economic participation and economic activities may be substantially undercounted, especially in rural areas.

In economies making the transition to a market economy, recent data on the percentages of females who are economically active are not readily available. However, women's participation in the labor force has traditionally been higher than in all other countries. In Russia, for example, women outnumbered men 52 to 48 in the labor force in 1991. In Eastern Europe, women accounted for 40–50 percent of the labor force, compared with 35–40 percent in Western Europe.

Working women earn less (per hour), on average, than working men in most countries. In Latin America and the Caribbean, for example, the ratio of women's to men's wages ranges from 60 percent in countries like Argentina, Bolivia, and Brazil to approximately 80 percent in Colombia, Mexico, and Panama. Evidence on total earnings (that is, monthly or quarterly) of men and women shows that the difference in earnings is even wider because of gender differences in hours worked in wage employment. Moreover, the earnings of women relative to men is higher for younger workers and lower for older workers (Figure 4). There is considerable evidence from many countries in Latin America and the Caribbean and in Asia that differences in human capital endowments (education, work experience, and so forth) between men and women explain only a small proportion of the wage differential. A study

Figure 3.   The Percentage of Economically Active Females, Aged 15 and over, Rose in Most Developing Countries between 1970 and 1990

Average percentage of economically active females

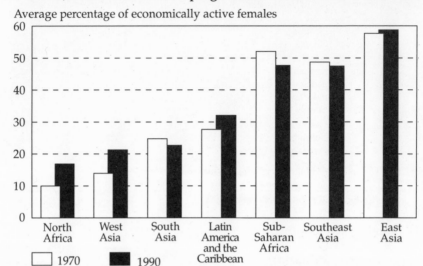

Source: United Nations Statistical Office 1991.

Figure 4.   Younger Women's Earnings Are Closer to Men's Than Are Older Women's Earnings

Ratio of females' to males' wages

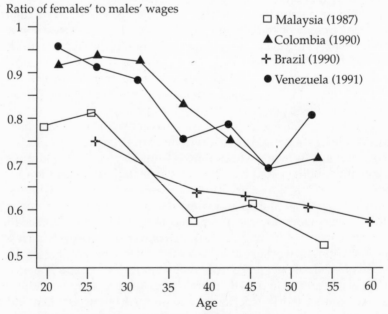

Source: Sedlacek, Gutierrez, and Mohindra 1993.

on fifteen Latin American and Caribbean countries documents that less than 25 percent of differentials in gender earnings during the period 1985–90 is related to human capital variables. Legal barriers and discriminatory hiring practices may explain much of the observed gender differences in earnings.

Progress in education and health is critical for human welfare—and for enhancing women's participation in development. Yet, the above analysis suggests that regions (and often countries within regions) differ in gender parity. Some countries and regions expanded their human resources and improved gender parity, whereas in others the human resource base expanded but gender parity did not improve. These contrasting patterns suggest that general progress in human resources is necessary but not sufficient for progress towards gender parity. Closing the gender gap requires positive public action to ensure that the average gains at the national level translate into gains for women as well as men.

2

The Payoffs to Investing in Women

Investing in women is critical for poverty reduction. It speeds economic development by raising productivity and promoting the more efficient use of resources; it produces significant social returns, improving child survival and reducing fertility; and it has considerable intergenerational payoffs.

Promoting Growth

Development and growth are best served when scarce public resources are invested where they yield the highest economic and social returns; indeed, social returns are, on the whole, greater for women than for men. Investing in women helps achieve these goals since the economic and social returns to such investments are high.

A growing body of research has established that the private *economic* rates of return to education are highest for primary education, more moderate for secondary education, and lower (but still considerable) for higher education.[2] The returns to schooling are considerable for *both* men and women—and in *all* regions of the developing world. Improving women's educational attainments contributes to their mobility from low-paying, low-productivity activities to activities of higher economic value.

Investing in women also produces major *social* returns central to development—for example, female education lowers fertility and slows population growth. Educated women desire fewer children and are better able to achieve their desired family size. Family planning programs reduce fertility more when combined with female education, especially in countries that have low female secondary enrollments. Moreover, since women's income-generating activities compete with childbearing

22

and childcare, increases in women's participation in the formal labor force are associated with smaller family size more than are increases in men's participation rates. In Brazil and Colombia—where labor force participation rates and earnings for men and women have been converging—fertility has been declining sharply.

Education, improved health, and access to income-generating activities for women do much to lower infant mortality and to improve child nutrition and survival. Even for a poor country with a GDP per capita of $300, a doubling of female secondary school enrollments (from 10 to 20 percent) would, controlling for all other factors, reduce the infant mortality rate from 105 deaths to 78 per 1,000 live births. The influence of women's education on infant deaths averted is thus far greater than that of direct intervention aimed at reducing mortality and fertility.

Improving women's health also improves the health of children and other family members. For example, about 24 million infants are born each year at low birth weights, largely because of their mothers' malnutrition during pregnancy, and about 5 million of these children die before reaching the age of five. Food supplementation for a malnourished pregnant woman can purchase an additional year of healthy life for her child for an estimated expenditure of only $25—and this estimate does not include the health benefits to the mother. A long-term study in the Matlab district of Bangladesh found that while the death of a father increased child mortality by 6 deaths per 1,000 children under five, regardless of the child's sex, a mother's death increased child mortality by 50 per 1,000 for boys and 144 per 1,000 for girls. Clearly, the social gains (externalities) from reducing premature deaths among adult women are very high.

Increasing the income in the hands of poor women through the expansion of employment opportunities is also associated with reduced child mortality and improved child health and nutrition. In India, where female mortality exceeds male mortality, district statistics and household surveys indicate that where the local labor market activity and income of adult women are greater than that of adult men, the survival rate for girls relative to boys is more equal. Also in India, women's participation in a major public works program in the Maharashtra state considerably improved the nutrition of their children. In most African countries, household food security is primarily the responsibility of women. So, raising the productivity of women in agriculture, absolutely and relative to their potential, is bound to contribute to better family nutrition, especially for the women's children, in addition to increasing household incomes.

One benefit of education for women themselves is a lower maternal mortality rate. Female education significantly reduces the risk associated with pregnancy and childbirth by increasing women's knowledge about health care practices and reducing the average number of pregnancies. Simulations suggest that an additional year of schooling for 1,000 women may prevent 2 maternal deaths. Poor nutrition in childhood and adolescence prevents many women from realizing their physical growth potential. A state-by-state national survey in India showed that between 15 and 29 percent of women aged 20–24 weighed less than 38 kilograms, and between 12 and 23 percent were shorter than 145 centimeters. Below these levels, women are at high risk of obstetric complications and death.

Calculations by the World Bank show that spending for improving health care for adult women aged 15–44 offers the biggest return of health care spending for any other demographic group of adults (men or women). The major causes of disability and premature death for women of reproductive age are treatable with low-cost interventions. Six of the ten main such causes for this group can be prevented or treated for less than $100 per year of healthy life gained, compared to three causes of illness for men (Table 4). These categories include illness associated with pregnancy, childbirth, respiratory infection, and anemia—which together account for 44 percent of the burden of disease among women of reproductive age. The marginal cost of providing a year of healthy life is smaller for this group than for any other adult population.

Table 4.   It Is Cost-Effective to Avoid Female Illness and Death: Health Intervention Priorities in Young Adults Aged 15–44

Rank	Male	Cost-effective Controls?	Rank	Female	Cost-effective Controls?
1	HIV	Y	1	Maternal	Y
2	Tuberculosis	Y	2	STDS	Y
3	Motor vehicle injuries	M	3	Tuberculosis	Y
4	Homicide and violence	n.a.	4	HIV	Y
5	War	n.a.	5	Depression	M
6	Self-induced injury	n.a.	6	Self-inflicted injury	n.a.
7	Depression	M	7	Respiratory	Y
8	Falls	n.a.	8	Anemia	Y
9	Alcohol dependence	n.a.	9	Osteoarthritis	n.a.
10	Respiratory infections	Y	10	Motor vehicle injuries	M

Y = Can be substantially controlled with less than $100 per DALY saved.
M = Can be partially controlled with $250–$999 per DALY saved.
n.a. = Interventions have not been evaluated for cost-effectiveness.
Note: DALY indicates the Disability-Adjusted Life Year, a measure that combines healthy life years lost because of premature mortality with those lost as a result of morbidity; STD means sexually transmitted diseases; and HIV is the human immunodeficiency virus.
Source: World Bank 1993a.

Promoting Efficiency

Education offers favorable private returns to the individual and has a long-term and sustainable effect on women's productivity and thus on the growth of the sector they work in. In countries such as India and Peru, in which modern agricultural technologies have been introduced, returns to an additional year of women's education range from 2 to 15 percent, comparable to those of men. Simulations in Kenya suggest that there may be significant gains from increasing women's physical and human capital to the levels of men's (Table 5).

Increasing the opportunities for women to participate in economically productive formal labor market activities also increases economic efficiency. Reducing wage differences between men and women—independently of their productive attributes—contributes to an economy's allocative efficiency. The apparent lower relative return to women's participation leads parents to invest less in girls' and women's education than in boys' and men's—a pattern perpetuated from one generation to another, prolonging and intensifying losses from inefficient investment in and allocation of productive and human resources.

In the former socialist economies of Eastern Europe and the Soviet Union, there were relatively fewer highly skilled jobs to be shared between men and women commensurate with their educational levels. However, the mismatch between education and job levels was higher for women than for men. In Russia, for example, 4.5 percent of all

Table 5. There Are Obvious Payoffs to Increasing the Human Capital of Women Farmers

Policy experiment	Increase in yields (percent)
Maize farmers, Kenya, 1976[a]	
Effect of giving female farmers age, education, and input levels of the average of all the individuals in the sample	7
Effect of giving female farmers men's age, education, and input levels	9
Effect of giving women primary schooling	24
Foodcrop farmers, Kenya, 1990[b]	
Effect of giving female farmers men's age, education, and input levels	22
Effect of increasing land area to male farmers' levels	10.5
Effect of increasing fertilizer to male farmers' levels	1.6

a. Coefficients from Moock 1976.
b. Coefficients from Saito, Mekonnen, and Spurling 1992; maize, beans, and cowpea production.
Source: Quisumbing 1993.

women in industry were in leadership positions, compared with 9 percent of all men. In some of the high-skill, technical sectors such as banking, insurance, information technology, the medical profession, and computing, women dominated; but their salary levels were lower than the average wage.

Reducing Poverty

Investing in women is a major theme of the Bank's two-pronged strategy for poverty reduction. This strategy calls for (a) broadly based, labor-absorbing economic growth to generate income-earning opportunities for the poor and (b) improved access to education, health care, and other social services to help the poor take advantage of these opportunities. Both components are designed to develop and use effectively the poor's most abundant asset—their labor. The weight of poverty falls most heavily on certain groups and women, in general, are disadvantaged. In poor households they often shoulder more of the workload than men, are less educated, and have less access to remunerative activities. They may spend long hours collecting water or firewood—time that could be used more productively if safe water and adequate fuel were close at hand. Investment in women—in their education and health and in opening access to resources and assets—strongly contributes to the two-pronged poverty reduction strategy. Moreover, women contribute a large share of household income for family survival. Evidence from diverse country settings—Burkina Faso, Cameroon, India, Lebanon, Nepal, and the Philippines—suggests that when the time spent on home production is valued and included in the computation of full household income, women contribute between 40 and 60 percent of household income. Raising the productivity and incomes of poor women is thus important for alleviating poverty.

Finally, to the extent that women are overrepresented among the poor, programs aimed at enhancing women's economic participation and productivity are highly compatible with targeted approaches to poverty reduction. In several African countries, women head more than one-third of families, suggesting that there is potential for reducing poverty by expanding income-earning opportunities for women. In some of the poorest countries, such as Bangladesh and India, encouraging the entrepreneurship and self-employment of women is proving to be a self-directed and targeted poverty reduction strategy. This is especially so because the formal sector cannot provide employment opportunities for the growing labor force. A recent comprehensive evaluation of Grameen Bank—a financial institution that provides credit to the poor, among whom women figure significantly—showed that its economic impact among participants was substantial, reducing poverty more than in nonparticipating villages. In Indonesia, lending under the KUPEDES (an acronym derived from the Indonesian words for Rural Credit) program of the Bank Rakyat Indonesia dropped the poverty ratio of first-time borrowers from 15 to 4 percent after three years of participation, as their incomes rose two-and-a-half times. There is also evidence that as women gain access to income, they shift their social position both inside and outside the family. To this extent, women's entrepreneurship is an "empowerment" strategy. Finally, social safety net interventions targeted at women are important for poverty reduction in those countries where women are hurt disproportionately because of inappropriate economic policies and the subsequent adjustment or transition.

Helping Future Generations

Educated mothers worldwide are better able to prepare their children for school and, later, for participation in technical and industrial sectors.

In developing countries—Colombia, Ghana, and Thailand among others—children of educated mothers perform better on preschool tests. An important study found that mothers' schooling was a significant determinant of children's schooling in Indonesia and the Philippines. Mothers' schooling also has a strong influence on their daughters' educational and occupational aspirations. In Malaysia, among Malays, a mother's education had a strong positive influence on her daughters' (but not on her sons') schooling, whereas the father's education generally did not affect his children's schooling. In Morocco, the school participation rate of rural girls increases by 55 percent when the household (male) head's education increases from none to primary level but by 135 percent when the (female) spouse's education changes from none to primary level. A study of university students in Egypt, Kuwait, and Lebanon found that daughters of educated mothers held fewer stereotypical sex-role attitudes than did daughters of nonliterate mothers.

Promoting Sustainable Development

Improving opportunities for women is critical for ensuring development compatible with environmental sustainability. Sustainable development requires easing population pressure and conserving natural resources, and women's decisions count heavily on both fronts. Population growth increases the *demand* for food. If traditional production practices continue, it also implies that additional *supplies* of food must come from excessive land use, which will lead to environmental degradation. Thus, in much of Sub-Saharan Africa, high population growth rates and agricultural stagnation have meant overgrazing, deforestation, and depletion of water resources. Arable land per person has also declined from 0.5 hectare in 1965 to 0.3 in 1987. Reducing population growth and raising agricultural productivity are *both* important for sustainable development. Investment in women—in education, in raising women farmers' productivity, and in promoting awareness of health and sanitation—can have significant effects in contributing to environmentally sustainable growth.

Women also have a vested interest in conserving natural resources because of their deep concern for the quality of the ecosystem. This concern is rooted in their daily reality, their experience as persons primarily responsible for obtaining fuel and water in much of the developing world, and their role in managing the consumption patterns of the household. It is also rooted in their concern for the future generations they bear. In addition, depletion of forest resources can have a severe effect on women's incomes because they are the primary gatherers of minor forest produce. Therefore promoting women's ownership and control of land, trees, and other forest resources and developing appropriate technologies (for example, light transport facilities for fuelwood, improved stoves, and the like) to reduce time women spend in collecting water and fuel can contribute to environmental sustainability.

Through their economic and household activities, women can have significant impacts on environmental quality and sustainable use of resources. For example, in traditional agricultural systems, women are responsible for collecting animal and crop residues, maintaining compost heaps, and applying organic fertilizers in their fields. Women's participation in decisions on such matters as the types and amounts of fertilizers and pesticides to be used have far-reaching implications on the environment. Women can also be instrumental in repairing environmental damage. Finally, women have considerable experience in managing the environment because they interact with it on a daily basis in the course of their household and economic activities.

3

The Barriers

Despite the developmental payoffs—in equity and efficiency—from investing in women, women still face many barriers in contributing to and benefiting from development.

Low Investments in Women's Education and Health

Schooling is never free and is seldom inexpensive, even when governments pay for much of it. In most countries, parents bear the direct costs for school fees, books, and clothing. Parents also incur opportunity costs because they lose their children's availability for chores and wage earnings. The poorer the family, the more difficult it is to bear these direct costs and the opportunity costs of education. Actual expenditures on schooling amount to about 4 percent of household consumption in low-income countries, 6 percent in middle-income countries, and 8 percent in industrial countries. For many reasons, especially because of cultural norms, these costs are often higher for girls than for boys; for example, parents' reluctance to send daughters to school without proper attire increases the cost of girls' schooling. Evidence from Morocco confirms that the direct costs to the family of sending girls to school exceed the direct costs of sending boys.

The same is true for the opportunity costs of educating children, which vary by sex and by country. In general, girls perform more chores at home than boys do: girls cook, clean, fetch water and wood, and care for younger siblings. Between the ages of 10 and 15, girls may work up to 8 to 10 hours a day on activities inside and outside the home. For example, in Malawi school-age girls spend more time on household chores than boys, and less time the first hour after school on relaxing. In Burkina Faso, girls 7 and older spend 3.5 hours a day on household tasks, compared with 1.5 hours for boys. In India, Bangladesh, and Nepal, girls by age 5 are involved in many household tasks and farm activities. A poor family cannot afford to forgo such help.

In many countries, underinvestment in girls' human capital is also a result of the school system's inability to meet parental preferences. For example, parents in many countries would like their girls to be taught by women, and a shortage of female teachers can inhibit girls' school attendance. In the Kerala state, which has the highest literacy and enrollment rates in India, more than 60 percent of teachers are women, compared with less than 20 percent in the states of Bihar and Uttar Pradesh, which have the lowest female enrollment rates. In rural areas, the shortage of female teachers is much worse. Poor roads, limited public transportation, and lack of teacher training institutions in rural areas hinder rural women from receiving teacher training. Not surprisingly, in Kerala road transport is highly developed, safe, and reliable, allowing female teachers from urban areas to travel long distances to teach in rural schools.

Although the costs of schooling to parents are real and immediate, the benefits often are not. The high private economic rates of return accrue to the individuals—the women themselves. Parents realize limited benefits from their children's education—and, in some countries, less from daughters than from sons. Investment in female education becomes an unattractive proposition to parents when the benefits do not accrue to the parents, especially when family budget constraints are overwhelming. So, families and societies tend to invest more in boys, who can produce and earn more, and whose earnings are retained in the family.

Low investment in the health of girls and women is apparent in many countries. Girls are often less cared for and more undernourished than boys, as reflected in higher age-specific mortality rates for girls and a low ratio of females to males in the population. This is especially marked in some South Asian countries. In many developing countries, more adult women than men are illiterate. Poor health and nutritional status, in turn, reduce girls' learning capability and cause wastage from high dropout rates. In a few countries in South Asia, the girls' biological advantage in early childhood is quickly eroded or reversed. Different allocations of food and medical care have been documented in several careful household studies, revealing discrimination in favor of boys over girls within the household. This is one of the many factors explaining the higher death rates among girls in the 1–4 year age group (Table 6). There is also evidence of discrimination against young girls in food and health care in many countries.

Table 6. More Girls Than Boys Die at a Young Age
(deaths per year per 1,000 population aged 1–4 years)

Country	Girls	Boys
Niger	232	212
Burundi	114	101
Togo	90	75
Cameroon	75	64
Guatemala	47	44
Egypt	36	25
Pakistan	36	22
Indonesia	35	36
Peru	31	29
Ecuador	26	25
Morocco	24	21
Dominican Republic	20	17
Mexico	16	14
Thailand	11	11
Sri Lanka	10	10
Colombia	6	11

Source: Compiled from Demographic and Health Surveys of different countries.

Low investments in women's education and health place women at a considerable disadvantage relative to men in the formal labor market. Many studies have shown that the probability of participation in the labor market increases with a woman's educational qualifications. In Argentina, the observed average participation for all women is 36 percent—22 percent for a woman with less than a primary education, but 58 percent for a university graduate.

The problems associated with transition from command economies to market economies in Eastern Europe and the former Soviet Union have received attention and analysis in the Bank. Women in these countries have generally high human capital endowments. Nevertheless, both before and after transition, women were disadvantaged, and women's condition generally worsened after the transition (Box 1). Addressing women's issues in Eastern Europe and the former Soviet Union , however, requires a different approach than that adopted in other developing countries. In the former command economies the problem is not to achieve gender parity in access to education and health services, but to maintain the progress already made. The issues of relevance to women in these countries include exploring cost-effective options for childcare, reinstating medical services and expanding contraceptive options for women, and ensuring that women adversely affected by transition are protected by safety nets as much as men are.

Box 1.   Profiles of Women in Eastern Europe and the Former Soviet Union (FSU)

Before the transition in Eastern Europe and the formal Soviet Union there was a conscious effort to integrate women in the economy by providing them with equal access to health and education. As a result, no gender disparity in school enrollments is observed. Nevertheless, women's health status was lower than might be expected for middle-income countries with high levels of female education and significant health infrastructure. For example, estimated maternal mortality ranges from 40 to 110 deaths per 100,000 live births in Kazakhstan, Moldova, Romania, the Russian Federation, and Turkmenistan compared with less than 20 deaths per 100,000 live births in other middle-income countries such as Costa Rica, and 10 deaths per 100,000 live births or less in western and northern Europe.

Since transition, the existing forms of female disadvantage have, if anything, intensified. The already weak reproductive health services—maternal and child health and contraception services—are in danger of being undermined further in the face of reductions in public resources following transition. Most women of reproductive age lack regular access to the range of modern methods of contraception. Between 1985 and 1990, the contraception prevalence rate varied from 7 percent in Azerbaijan to 26 percent in Estonia, compared with 76 percent in the Netherlands and 81 percent in the United Kingdom. Abortion remains almost the only available method of fertility control. Deteriorating health conditions are being reflected in large percentages of anemia among pregnant women, iodine and iron deficiencies, and high incidences of cardiovascular, respiratory, and noncommunicable diseases. According to WHO estimates, in Uzbekistan 70 percent of pregnant women may suffer from anemia, and the percentage may be even higher in rural areas.

Prior to transition, women participated fully in the labor market, and childcare facilities were provided by the enterprises. Women now make up 70 to 80 percent of the total unemployed, and they stay unemployed for longer periods of time than men do in some countries. Childcare facilities are threatened by enterprise restructuring and privatization. For example, in Poland in the 1980s the number of factory-run nurseries decreased by a quarter, the number of places by a third, and the number of children in nurseries by almost half. The closure of traditional childcare institutions during transition puts an especially heavy burden on single mothers. Younger women are consciously forgoing career opportunities in favor of maternal duties.

Thus, notwithstanding the generally higher human capital endowments, women in Eastern Europe and the FSU were disadvantaged before the transition and continue to be in a weaker position after the transition.

Source: Tinker and Godinho 1994; Godinho 1994; WHO 1992; Moghadam 1993.

Poor Access to Services and Assets

Education

Not having a school within easy reach of home is an important barrier to girls' enrollment. In Ghana, the long distance to school deters girls' enrollment more than boys'. In Morocco, a paved road increases a girl's probability of ever attending a school by 40 percent—and reduces her probability of dropping out by 5 percent. Too often, girls do not go to school unless the school offers separate lavatories and girls' common rooms. In some cultures, girls' participation in school depends on whether girls' schools are available.

Health services

A significant barrier to better health for women is the lack of access to the means for planning the number and timing of pregnancies, and for safely ending unwanted pregnancies where that is legal. Women in the reproductive years are exposed to dangers associated with pregnancy and childbirth, and they experience the heavy nutritional demands of reproduction and lactation at the same time that their work loads in the marketplace and household are heaviest. Their vulnerability is particularly high if they have been undernourished in childhood and adolescence.

In all developing countries, the incidence of HIV/AIDS is increasing more rapidly among women than men; in some countries, more than half of those infected are women. Women's low social status and economic dependence often interfere with their ability to obtain information about and treatment for AIDS and other sexually transmitted diseases—and their ability to negotiate for safer sexual practices to reduce their vulnerability.

Despite their high burden of disease, women in developing countries face great obstacles in seeking and obtaining health care. One World Bank country study concluded that women's use of health services depended on a combination of four factors: need, permission, ability, and availability. *Need* is a measure for the demand for health services; *permission* and *ability* are measures of effective demand, reflecting the social and economic constraints on women's behavior. Many women face substantial social inhibitions in traveling to a medical facility, seeing a male doctor, seeking family planning services, or even addressing their own health concerns. Their ability to take advantage of health care—even when such social constraints are overcome—may be limited by the direct and indirect costs of care. The *availability* of health resources reflects the supply side of the equation and may be a fundamental constraint on health-seeking behavior for both men and women.

Water and sanitation

In spite of women's significant role in managing household water and sanitation, a variety of barriers, often relating to location, design, staffing, and scheduling issues, reduce women's access to services. The siting of facilities may not recognize gender differences relating to mobility around the village. For example, in parts of India where female seclusion is practiced, women continued to use nearby polluted water sources rather than walk to improved facilities far from their homes. Again in India, compost pits located outside villages remained unused, and women continued to deposit refuse near their homes, as it was not acceptable for women to be seen carrying loads of refuse to the outskirts of the village. Another barrier can arise where women cannot meet with male staff or where the timing, duration, and location of meetings and training do not take women's needs into account, thereby reducing their access to the facilities.

Adequate facilities can, if used correctly, improve the health of women and their families. Facilities that are close by also reduce the time women and girls spend obtaining water. This may facilitate girls' attendance at school and women's involvement in income-generating activities. Women are most often the collectors, users, and managers of water in the household, and they may have community management roles as well. Because of this, women have considerable knowledge about sanitation practices and about water sources, including quality and reliability, restrictions, acceptable storage methods, and so on, and this knowledge can be an important input for project design. Women's preferences should be taken into account, as a system that does not meet their needs may not be used and may fall into disuse.

Agricultural services and sustainable use of resources

Despite women's important role as farm managers and agricultural workers (whether as family or hired laborers) their access to extension services has not equaled that of male farmers. Traditional extension systems—based on single-commodity extension—often fail to consider women's crops and activities such as beans, maize, cowpeas, sorghum, and livestock rearing. General extension, by contrast, covers the broad spectrum of women's activities, but the range of tasks covered may limit the time devoted to any single task. Furthermore, extension systems in many developing countries are overloaded; agent-farmer ratios in Africa, Asia, the Middle East and North Africa, and Latin America range from one agent to 2,000 or even 3,000 farmers. In contrast, an extension agent in Europe and North America serves between 300 and 400 farmers.

Women are also underrepresented among extension agents. Even in regions with a long tradition of female farming, such as Africa, only 11 percent of the extension staff and 7 percent of the field extension staff are women. Whereas female extension workers may be trained in agriculture, they are mandated to give advice on home economics subjects. This may constrain the delivery of agricultural extension messages to female farmers, who may be restricted from interacting with male extension agents and who prefer to interact with female agents.

In several African countries, male farmers have greater contact with the extension service than do female farmers (Table 7). Evidence from Burkina Faso, Malawi, and Zambia also shows that extension advice to one member of a family frequently is not passed on to the person who carries out the task.

Similar barriers exist in the conservation of natural resources. Environmental stress (land conversion, soil fertility, and deforestation), in and of itself, can be an important factor that undermines women's ability to use and manage resources wisely. For example, conversions of land to alternative uses such as roads or commercial, agriculture, and industrial development may push women on to more marginal lands that become even more degraded because women have no alternative but to farm them to meet their subsistence food needs. Social and institutional factors such as lack of access to land and information may also undermine women's ability to maintain environmental quality and sustainable use of resources. For example, persuading women to grow trees and participate in social forestry projects is difficult if they do not have land on which to grow trees or if they are not guaranteed ownership of the fruit and timber. Even in countries where recent reforms may acknowledge the rights to common lands, women's access to land may be inadequately protected by the legal and administrative systems. Lack of education and training often prevent women from contributing effectively to sound environmental management and from participating fully in environment projects. Women's access to training tends to be

Table 7. Extension Agents Visit More Men Than Women
(percentage of families)

Country and year	Male-headed household	Female-headed household
Kenya, 1989	12	9
Malawi, 1989	70	58
Nigeria, 1989	37	22
Tanzania, 1984	40	28
Zambia, 1982	57	29
Zambia, 1986	60	19

Source: Quisumbing 1993.

limited because forest extension services and programs may ignore them or because there is insufficient female staff to train them.

Credit

Lack of access to credit—both formal and informal—is another major barrier, often restricting women's ability to smooth consumption over time and undertake productive activities. Evidence from Côte d'Ivoire and Kenya suggests that women have a lower likelihood of borrowing from formal sources and even from other individuals because of collateral requirements, high transaction costs, limited education and mobility, social and cultural barriers, and the nature of women's businesses.

Property that is acceptable as collateral, especially land, is usually in men's names, and the valuables women own (such as jewelry) are often deemed unacceptable by formal financial institutions. The transaction costs in obtaining credit—for transport, paperwork, time spent waiting, and so on—may be higher for women because of higher opportunity costs from forgone activities. In rural Kenya, the distance to a bank is a significant determinant of women's probability of obtaining credit, but it does not affect men's borrowing behavior. Women's lower educational levels, coupled with social and cultural barriers, may constrain their mobility and their interaction with predominantly male credit officers. And women tend to be involved in relatively low-value crops not covered by crop-related credit programs.

The barriers that women—especially poor women—face in obtaining and using financial services are closely related to their gender roles. Socially and culturally defined roles and responsibilities influence the kinds of business activities that are most likely to engage women and restrict their ability to take advantage of conventional banking and credit facilities. Seclusion, illiteracy, and lack of title to land or other assets reduce women's access to formal credit. Heavy responsibilities for care and provisioning in the household restrict women's working hours and mobility in ways that affect their choice of sector and of business practices. Women's businesses thus tend to be smaller—and grow slower—than men's. They are more likely to be home based and to be in sectors that are technologically unsophisticated and overcrowded to the point of market saturation. These business characteristics mean that women entrepreneurs are perceived as poor credit risks.

Legal and Regulatory Barriers

Legal and regulatory barriers prevent women in some countries from fully participating in formal labor markets. For example, legal restrictions that forbid women to enter contracts in their own name may bar women from some lines of work. A study of six countries in the Middle East (Egypt, Jordan, Kuwait, Morocco, Turkey, and Tunisia) found that labor laws forbade women to engage in night work and dangerous work, though the definitions and categories vary across the countries. Even in some transitional economies, labor laws prohibit women's employment in certain occupations. Such laws may have been instituted to protect women workers, reflecting the existing cultural norms—but in practice they may actually reduce women's participation.

In many countries, patriarchal traditions and loopholes in legislation prevent equalization of inheritance rights. In some Southeast Asian countries (for example, Indonesia, the Philippines, and Thailand), by contrast, women can own, inherit, acquire, and dispose of property in their own right. Even in these countries, however, practice can differ, despite provisions for equality of inheritance between sons and daughters under civil law.

Under customary law in many African countries, women usually had rights to some land, which was allocated to women from their husbands and natal families on the basis of their position within a kinship group and, in particular, on their relationship to a father, brother, or husband. These rights entitled women to farm the land, often in exchange for labor on their husbands' plots and other family plots. Western colonization modified these indigenous customs by introducing private ownership and individual registration of land, often discriminating against women. Furthermore, since women usually obtained land rights through a male relative, there was no guarantee that they would retain these rights after a husband's death or divorce.

The absence of formal land rights and the smaller plots of land cultivated by women are critical, since land is usually needed as collateral in credit markets. A farm household survey in Kenya and Nigeria found that more male than female heads of households, and more male than female farmers, were able to exercise their land rights fully. The ability of women to exercise the full range of land rights—to sell or mortgage the land—is essential to the equitable functioning of land markets.

Women's Dual Roles at Home and in the Marketplace

Women frequently have to withdraw from the labor market because of the demands of marriage and children. Women are therefore more likely to choose jobs that allow them greater flexibility in hours worked. This often brings a drop in earnings, often associated with a shift from wage work to self-employment in the informal sector. Women also lag behind men in the accumulation of human capital as a result of discontinuity in employment.

Practical constraints impede women's work outside the home and restrict women from securing higher-paying jobs. The lack of cost-effective childcare is a major barrier for working women in developing countries. In a survey in Egypt, 92 percent of the women were of the opinion that more women would join the labor force if better childcare facilities were available. In the absence of affordable childcare facilities, working women have no option but to alter the amount and type of market work they engage in so that they can to balance it with household responsibilities. For example, a study in Lima found that women without children or with one child tend to work in the wage sector, while women with two or more children are likely to be self-employed.

As the number of dependent children increases, women tend to drop out of the labor force, demonstrating a tradeoff between market work and childcare. This barrier is less onerous in countries where extended families predominate. In many African and South Asian economies, children are not a major barrier to the female labor market participation, and childbearing does not reduce the potential duration of the working life of females relative to males. However, the physical demands of childbearing and childcare make it harder for women and girls to seek education, training, and employment away from home.

In many settings, the absence of piped water or readily available cooking fuel makes it necessary to spend many hours obtaining them—tasks most commonly considered by society to be women's responsibility. After meeting these and other time-consuming household responsibilities, many women have little time or energy to devote to income-generating activities.

In the economies of the former Soviet Union and Eastern Europe that are making the transition to a market economy, women are beginning to face obstacles in the labor market similar to those elsewhere. In these countries, prior to transition, there were extensive crèche facilities for working mothers, who were also entitled to take leave to care for sick children. Since restructuring, some crèche facilities have closed because governments or state enterprises can no longer afford to operate them, and this situation adversely affects employment prospects for women.

4

Operational Experience

The experience of the past two decades suggests some promising approaches to overcoming the barriers to improving women's status and productivity (Box 2). Evidence on "what works" in a given situation—and whether an intervention is cost-effective—is stronger in some areas than others. However, the experience accumulated in some core areas suggests that closing the gender gap with respect to key socioeconomic indicators is a realizable goal—even for very poor developing countries. That experience from World Bank and country operations, other donors' work, and nongovernmental organizations' (NGOs) activities points unambiguously to five main operational strategies for improving women's status and productivity:

- Expanding girls' enrollments
- Improving women's health
- Increasing women's participation in the formal labor force
- Expanding women's options in agriculture
- Providing financial services to women.

Much of the operational experience so far gained is inevitably country-specific. The purpose of reviewing the experience is not to draw generalizations applicable to all countries and situations but to highlight what works in a given situation to ensure more favorable gender outcomes. Before experience gained in one country is replicated in another country, it is imperative to identify the issues and the socioeconomic milieu of the first country and then suitably to adapt and to apply only the relevant lessons of experience.

Expanding Girls' Enrollments

For expanding girls' enrollments, a basic policy instrument is to increase school places so that schools are within reach. If there are too few school

39

Box 2. The Evolution of the World Bank's Involvement in Gender Issues

The Bank's first efforts to address women in development were in the late 1960s and were pushed forward in the Bank's agenda under the initiative of the United Nations Decade for Women. In 1977 the Bank created the post of adviser on women in development to increase attention to women's issues in the Bank's activities. Initially, the focus was on sensitizing Bank staff to the role of women in development and gathering data and information about women's status.

Toward the end of the Decade for Women, the Bank embarked on a more ambitious initiative. This thrust was formalized in 1987 with the establishment of the Women in Development Division in the central Population and Human Resources Department and the designation of women in development (WID) as one of the Bank's areas of special emphasis. In 1990 the effort was decentralized when regional WID coordinator positions were created. Attention to women's issues became more explicitly justified on the basis of economic growth as well as welfare, with a focus on increasing women's productivity in agriculture, opening labor markets to women, and improving women's access to family planning, health, and education.

Efforts to increase knowledge of women's roles, constraints, and contributions to the development process were accelerated under a mandate that required each region to produce Women's Country Assessment Reports. About forty such assessments have been prepared and discussed with the respective governments. The Bank has also addressed WID issues in country economic memoranda, poverty assessments, and other economic and sector work. In addition, a number of special studies have focused on regional WID issues, particularly with respect to human capital formation and employment.

Policy and research work include papers on examples of best practices in the area of education, agriculture, forestry, women's health, and credit for the poor. These papers have documented the economic and social benefits that result from addressing WID issues in these areas, and suggest operational strategies for enhancing women's contribution to development. A retrospective study on the Bank's experience is under preparation by the Bank's Operations Evaluation Department.

---

places, the scarce places often are first allocated to boys. Another basic policy instrument is to reserve some school places for girls. In Malawi the government reserves a third of all secondary school places for girls, and a Bank-assisted project to build secondary schools resulted in higher female enrollments than expected. Tanzania has a similar policy.

For promoting literacy among adult women, however, different policies, such as expansion of nonformal educational facilities, would be needed. Experience with reference to the impact of such policies on adult female literacy is very limited.

Bangladesh, Chad, India, Pakistan, Senegal, and Yemen have made special efforts to expand classrooms or build new schools exclusively for girls. Evidence shows that in a variety of cultures girls' enrollment and performance improve if they attend single-sex rather than coeducational schools in a variety of cultures. In densely populated countries, single-sex schools can alleviate parental concerns about girls' safety and improve girls' performance, and the unit costs may not be high. Care should be taken, however, that there are no differences in school curriculum and that single-sex schools prepare girls adequately in science and mathematics.

Locating schools closer to children's homes seems promising because of parental concern about girls' personal safety. This step can also reduce the direct costs of transportation and boarding for girls. Project experience suggests that having more and smaller schools with closer ties to the community is effective for boys as well as girls. Nonformal schools run by the Bangladesh Rural Advancement Committee (BRAC) and satellite schools, located in the community and within walking distance, have high attendance and retention rates for girls. Morocco is also providing small local schools for middle-level education.

Female teachers can draw more girls into school—even in a coeducational setting. Cross-country data suggest a strong positive correlation between the parity of enrollment for boys and girls and the proportion of female teachers. The main problem in some countries is the lack of female teachers, especially in rural areas. Initiatives in projects to overcome the shortage of female teachers include implementing a quota system to recruit more female teachers, removing age restrictions, introducing local recruitment and posting, and building teacher-training institutions in rural areas. Experience from Bangladesh, Nepal, and Pakistan suggests that it is not hard to find good female teachers if required training is provided and women teachers are posted near their homes. The combination of locally recruited and motivated female teachers and active in-service training and supervision can reduce the shortage of female teachers in rural areas. Ongoing Bank projects in Bangladesh, China, India, Nepal, Pakistan, and Yemen are trying such strategies to increase the proportion of female teachers.

A minimum of physical infrastructure appears necessary to attract and retain girls in school. Some projects in Bangladesh and Pakistan are providing separate sanitary facilities and constructing boundary walls around girls' schools.

Evidence from Bangladesh, Egypt, Mali, Morocco, Peru, Tunisia, and Yemen also suggests, however, that supplying adequate school places and school facilities is not sufficient if the demand for girls' education is low because of other constraints—such as, for example, books, clothing, time needed to do house chores and to care for siblings. For school places to be fully used, demand for girls' education must emanate from parents and the community.

One way of increasing demand is to lower both direct and opportunity costs. Some education projects have cut these costs by waiving or reducing fees, supplying free textbooks, providing scholarships or stipends for girls, offering flexible school hours, and establishing childcare centers. These approaches not only reduce the costs to parents, but also improve school quality, reduce dropout rates, improve the efficiency of the school system, and significantly increase girls' effective participation.

Bangladesh has experienced success with a scholarship program for girls living in rural areas. The program, started in one area in 1977 by the Bangladesh Association for Community Education (a local NGO) as a means of delaying marriage by keeping girls in school, now covers seven areas and is administered by six NGOs. Girls' secondary enrollments and attendance have increased and their dropout rates have decreased. Encouraged by the results, in 1990 the government began experimenting with a free-tuition-for-girls policy to attract more rural girls into grades 6–8. Two Bank projects in Bangladesh currently provide stipends for secondary school girls, including funds for tuition, textbooks, stationery, uniforms, snacks, and transport.

A Guatemala NGO's scholarship program for primary school girls, modeled after the one in Bangladesh, began in 1987 with one village and later expanded to twelve villages. Since parents pay no tuition and schoolbooks are free, the monthly scholarship payment partly compensates parents for other school-related expenses and for the loss of their daughters' time. More than 90 percent of the scholarship girls are completing primary schooling, and the Guatemalan government is planning to fund new scholarships for eleven more communities.

In assessing the benefits of projects involving components for ensuring gender parity (such as scholarships for girls), it is important to include the economic gains of savings in internal efficiency. Perhaps even more important are the social gains (externalities) from postponing the age of marriage for girls and the longer-term impacts from a lower fertility rate. A recent study for Pakistan suggests that the externalities from female education can be considerable. An additional year of school for 1,000 women, at a total cost of $30,000, is estimated to increase wages by 20 percent and prevent 60 child deaths, 500 births, and three maternal deaths (Table 8).

Table 8. The Social Gains of Investing in Girls Are Enormous

Item	Calculation	Cost or benefit (U.S. dollars)
Recurrent cost of one year of education for 1,000 women		30,000
Benefits		
Reduction in child mortality		
Total averted deaths	60	
Set cost (U.S. dollars)	800	
Value of averted deaths		48,000
Reduction in fertility		
Births averted	500	
Set cost (U.S. dollars)	65	
Value of births averted		32,500
Reduction in maternal mortality		
Total maternal deaths averted	3	
Set cost (U.S. dollars)	2,500	
Value of averted maternal deaths		7,500

Source: Summers 1992.

Siting childcare centers at or near schools can free many girls to attend school. Provision of childcare relieves girls from sibling care during the day and can help improve the nutritional status and school readiness of younger siblings. In Columbia, where single mothers head one-fifth of the poorest households and 44 percent of poor children between the ages of 7 and 11 do not attend school, the community day-care program has freed many girls and women to attend school or join the work force. China, too, has established day-care centers at schools and worksites, improving girls' enrollment in urban areas. A Bank-financed general education project in Bangladesh also included day-care provision for younger siblings in satellite schools.

Childcare problems of women are often accentuated by divorce laws that do not provide adequate financial support from fathers and by lack of access of poor women to the courts to enforce such support. Clearly, it is important to reduce such legal barriers.

Another way to reduce the opportunity cost of girls' time to parents—at no cost—is to adjust school hours so that girls can more easily combine schooling with chores. This approach in nonformal educational programs in many countries has worked well. In India in the early 1980s a nonformal evening education program, staffed by teachers drawn from the local community, brought school dropouts back to the primary education mainstream and gave out-of-school children another chance. A Bank-supported project in Nepal has incorporated literacy and numeracy training at flexible times for adult women as well as primary school-age children (boys and girls) who have not benefited from the formal education system.

Another cost-effective means of reducing schedule conflicts for women is distance education, which generally involves a combination of radio and correspondence techniques. Radio (or sometimes television) is used for transmitting classroom instruction in all subjects, and students supplement this with the use of textbooks and self-paced workbooks. The world's largest educational institution, the Chinese Television University uses this model for postsecondary instruction, and the Malawi Correspondence College uses it at the secondary level. Evidence suggests that self-study schools can reduce costs by at least 20 to 30 percent while opening access to girls.

Measures outside the education sector can also reduce the opportunity costs of girls' time and promote female schooling. In Nepal, the government distributed fuel-efficient, smokeless, wood-burning stoves to 15,000 families as part of a program to check deforestation. The unintended externality of the program was to reduce the time girls spend in collecting wood for cooking, which may also translate into increased girls' enrollments. In Morocco girls' school enrollments were significantly higher in communities with tapped water than elsewhere.

Improving Women's Health

Avoidable female deaths in the developing countries are strongly associated with health care and nutrition failures, whereas avoidable male mortality is associated more with behavioral and occupational hazards that are less susceptible to prevention within the health sector, such as exposure to toxins, smoking, drug and alcohol use, violence, and accidents. The low marginal costs of preventing women's disability, illness, and premature death through family planning, nutritional supplementation, community-based primary health care, and safe motherhood programs (including safe abortion) argue for expanding such programs in *all* countries, especially in high-mortality, high-fertility settings. In Romania, the Bank's Health Rehabilitation Project has as its immediate objective the task of rehabilitating and upgrading the primary health care delivery system. This would include reproductive health care services focusing on maternal and child health and on increasing access and choice in family planning.

Health services that integrate nutrition training and supplementation, family planning, maternal and childcare, and primary health care are the most effective in reaching women because they address a wide spectrum of women's needs and responsibilities and save them time. In some settings, the training of female health personnel may be particularly important, and combining care for women and children can help overcome some of the permission barriers that inhibit women from seeking health care. A successful project in Tunisia offered family planning advice to women at the 100-day checkup of their newborn infants, reaching women who might not have presented themselves for family planning counseling alone.

Within integrated community-based programs, certain specific interventions have demonstrated particularly high payoffs for women's health. Well-designed distribution of iron folate tablets to adolescent girls and women of reproductive age can cheaply address one of the major causes of disability and death in this age group. Iodine fortification or supplementation in areas where deficiency is endemic will improve reproductive outcomes. Targeted food supplements for malnourished pregnant women protect them against the nutritional demands of pregnancy and maternal depletion and can improve child health outcomes cost-effectively.

Community-based outreach for health and family planning services is a cost-effective complement to facility-based primary health care systems, which is often underused because of difficulties of access and permission. In Albania, the Health Rehabilitation Project places strong emphasis on primary care and maternity and childcare services as having the highest returns to health investments. In Kenya, NGOs developed a network of such services and increased the impact of the primary health care system substantially, with only a modest increase in the total cost of the program. The impact was particularly large for family planning, with demand tripling in the program period. The study concluded that investment in community-based services is almost certainly highly cost-effective, in part because it results in more efficient use of medical facilities. The Safe Motherhood Initiative estimates that a basic, satisfactory system of primary care can be put in place for about $2.00 per capita a year (Box 3).

Legislation of abortion is a societal decision. Policies with respect to abortion, however, have implications for women's health. Romania's experience suggests that making abortion illegal can have very high costs in morbidity, mortality, and health care resources (Box 4). But even where abortion is legal and safe, inexpensive techniques are not always available. Where abortion is legal, community-based outreach for health and family planning services should include methods for safe abortion.

Because child survival is strongly correlated with the mother's education, interventions in the education sector have a strong impact on health. An all-India household survey showed that child survival was higher—90 percent—in families in which the mother had six or more years of education—90 percent—than in families of the highest income group—86 percent.

Box 3. The Safe Motherhood Initiative

The difference in maternal mortality rates between developing and industrial countries is the largest discrepancy observed for any human development indicator. In each pregnancy, women in developing countries face a risk of dying that is as much as 200 times greater than the risk faced by women in the industrial world, and because women in developing countries experience many more pregnancies, their comparative lifetime risk of dying in childbirth or from related causes is even more elevated.

The Safe Motherhood Initiative was launched in 1987 in an international effort to address the problem of maternal mortality. Cosponsored by the World Bank, the World Health Organization, the United Nations Fund for Population Activities, and agencies from more than forty-five countries, the initiative has as its objective the reduction of the number of maternal deaths worldwide (currently about 500,000 per year) by one-half by the year 2000.

Research and pilot projects have identified the essential components of safe motherhood as a series of interlinked steps, beginning with good nutrition for adolescent girls and continuing with information and education about reproductive health. Community-based public health measures such as family planning services, prenatal and postpartum care, training and deployment of midwives, and treatment for risk factors such as anemia, hypertension, and sexually transmitted diseases are also essential elements. Input from the community served, and especially from women, raises the chances of success in designing and managing effective programs.

The most important determinant of maternal mortality, however, is the management of actual complications associated with pregnancy—labor and delivery, incomplete abortions, obstructed labor, hemorrhage, toxemia, and infection. To reduce maternal mortality, access to health care facilities with the technical capacity and skills to intervene is required. So are the ability to recognize serious complications at an early stage and the availability of emergency transport to clinical facilities. Even community-based systems that function well with trained midwives in place can do only a limited amount to reduce maternal mortality if they do not have the backup capacity of some medical treatments such as vacuum aspiration, blood transfusions, and caesarian sections.

Significant reduction of maternal mortality requires systematic effort, but it can be managed with limited resources. Nonetheless, progress in reducing maternal mortality has been very slow.

The projected costs for achieving the goals outlined in the Safe Motherhood Initiative are approximately $2.00 per capita per year—half for maternal health and half for family planning. According to World Bank data, these are among the most cost-effective interventions known for improving the health of women and their children.

Source: Tinker, Koblinsky, and Daly 1993.

Box 4. The Effects of Legalizing Abortion

Romania offers a striking illustration of the impact of abortion laws on women's health. In 1966, the government—concerned about falling birth rates—outlawed both contraception and abortion. Enforcement was strict. By 1970, the maternal mortality rate was 40 percent above the level of 1965. By 1989, Romania's rate—which was similar to that of the other European countries in 1966—was ten times the level of any other European country's. In 1990 a new government restored the legality of abortion. One year later, maternal mortality had fallen to just 40 percent of its level in 1989.

Source: World Bank 1993a.

Several steps can be taken to facilitate women's access to water and sanitation services. The key is to involve women early in the project process. Gender analysis will indicate which barriers are relevant to women in the project area. Men and women can indicate the barriers as well as suggest ways to reduce or eliminate them. For example, facilities should be sited where women have easy access to them. Local norms may preclude women's access to, for example, areas far from the village. The design of facilities should take women's preferences into account.

Gender analysis will also reveal women's and men's different roles in water and sanitation. This knowledge can be used in designing appropriate interventions. For example, in one part of Ghana some families considered water to be women's responsibility and therefore expected women to pay pump tariffs. In this context it is especially important to discuss with women what type of facility they want and are willing to pay for. The timing, duration, and location of training must be tailored to fit women's schedules and needs, taking into account women's multifaceted roles. Furthermore, the proposed interventions should not unduly increase women's workloads. For example, although improved water systems that are conveniently located may reduce the amount of time women spend collecting water, they may create new demands for women's work relating to maintenance, management, and financing.

Increasing Women's Participation in the Formal Labor Force

Unlike the strategies in education and health, those for increasing the participation rates of women *and* reducing wage differences between men and women are less proven. The main strategies here include increasing the productivity of women, reducing the constraints women face while participating in the labor market, and improving the efficiency of the labor market.

Providing childcare can reduce the household constraints that working women face, particularly in urban areas where the extended family often is not available to help. With broader childcare facilities available, women may not need to compromise on the type of jobs they accept. This would also begin to bridge the male-female differences in earnings that cannot be attributed to human capital differences. The Community Childcare project in Colombia provides for the nutrition, health, and early-childhood development needs of children aged 2 through 6 in low-income urban communities. "Community mothers," chosen by parents, care for about fifteen children each in their homes. The service-support component of the project provides training to the community mothers and helps upgrade their homes to reach minimum standards for providing childcare. It increases the productive potential of mothers by offering alternative childcare arrangements, but its cost-effectiveness has yet to be evaluated.

Removing policies of segregation and discrimination to promote access to jobs and making information available to lower the search costs associated with finding a job are other strategies. The Employment and Training Project in Turkey incorporates some of these actions, but it is too recent to provide insights about their effectiveness. In the ongoing projects in Turkey and Hungary and in the forthcoming Romania project, youth and adult counseling systems and career awareness are intended to be gender neutral.

To ensure gender neutrality in job vacancies, the abolition of gender preferences can be specified as a project goal, as in the Turkey employment project. In countries where there is gender segregation, training projects for women could be designed to be more gender sensitive and address segregation issues. And where equal employment laws exist, countries can be encouraged to enforce them more rigorously.

Expanding the Options in Agriculture and Managing Natural Resources

The many responsibilities of rural women can impose time and energy constraints on their participation in programs designed to increase their incomes. Part of the strategy, therefore, is to increase their productivity in existing tasks. However, given the option, many women want to escape the drudgery of many of these activities, highlighting the importance of increasing women's options in agriculture and in home production.

Many projects of the Bank and other agencies include three basic interventions to improve the delivery of extension services to rural women. One is to improve the delivery of appropriate extension messages to women as a separate clientele. The second is to increase the number of female agents and supervisors in the extension system or to train male agents to work with female farmers. The third is to provide separate facilities, transportation, and other resources for extension to women farmers.

Delivering appropriate extension messages to women may entail revising the content and orientation of extension in order to address women farmers' needs. Technical training in Chile has traditionally been directed to men under the assumption that they are the target for such training. However, research has shown that women have good knowledge of agronomic practices, participate actively in farm decision-making, and even have higher literacy rates than males in rural areas, suggesting the potential for disseminating more complex technical messages. Under the Chile Small Farmers' Services Project, a team of private female consultants (agronomists and sociologists) trains regional technology-transfer teams to reorient extension methods and practices to serve rural women better. In a pilot project in Côte d'Ivoire, women eagerly approached female extension agents for advice on farming practices but were less enthusiastic regarding home economics courses. In extension systems staffed mostly by men, or for which it is difficult to recruit qualified women, male extension agents may also need to be trained to work with female clients, with a concomitant revision of extension methodology.

In countries where social norms restrict interaction between male agents and female farmers, gender-sensitive agricultural extension projects have deliberate provisions for increasing the number of female agents. The increased number of female agents can either be part of a unified extension system, as in Nigeria, or be an independent extension system, with separate facilities, under the overall extension service (Yemen), with the possibility of mainstreaming into the regular extension service in the future.

Special provisions can facilitate the delivery of extension messages by female agents to women farmers For example, female village group technicians can be taught to train women's groups, and qualified and interested wives of male agents can be trained to carry out extension functions on a part-time basis, as in the Turkey extension project. Since it is often difficult to recruit female agents for rural assignments, many projects recruit in the local area, recruit in pairs, and provide special allocations for housing and transportation (such as a car and driver for every two female technicians).

In societies that proscribe interaction between men and women, the provision of separate facilities for women may increase their participation in more remunerative employment. The India sericulture program, for example, provides separate spaces for women in cocoon markets and separate sanitary facilities in public spaces. Separate training centers for women were also built for the Yemen agricultural extension program.

Women bear the burden of environmental degradation, as they have to trek long distances to fetch fuelwood and water. Natural resource management projects and policy-oriented studies need to fully evaluate the costs and adverse externalities of environmental damage by including the direct and indirect costs to women's activities. Deforestation, for example, imposes both direct and opportunity costs on women. Direct costs result when fuelwood resources are depleted (and must be purchased), and indirect costs occur when women have to walk long distances to obtain fuelwood.

Women can be trained to contribute to environmental conservation. Such training in research and analysis of environmental problems and their causes and consequences can equip women to participate effectively in decisionmaking on issues relating to environmental policy. Technology transfer, if appropriately designed and adapted, could lead to more efficient use of resources, yield significant environmental benefits, and enhance women's productivity and ability to use resources more sustainably. For example, in Nepal, energy-efficient, nonpolluting cook stoves could not only reduce total energy consumption and pollution levels but could also yield additional benefits to women in time savings and health improvements. In all cases, women should have equal access to training and to the processes for setting priorities and for decisionmaking.

Natural resource management projects need to identify and consult women's groups in order to ensure environmental conservation and sustainable management. Failure to identify and acknowledge the role of women in environmental processes can result in inappropriate interventions and jeopardize the success of environmental projects. Wherever women play a role in influencing policymaking on environment, investigators could document and learn from experience. Women's groups and environmental NGOs can also play an important role (Box 5).

Providing Financial Services

High transaction costs, high perceived risks of default, a lack of collateral, and social resistance commonly bar women's access to credit (Box 6). One way to reduce transaction costs is group lending, in which members accept joint liability for loans. This relieves the lender of the costly process of checking the creditworthiness of individual borrowers

---

Box 5. Examples of Women's Participation in Natural Resource Conservation and Management

- In a small village in the Bankura district of West Bengal, India, a unique experiment, spearheaded by local women, has had a widespread impact in regenerating wastelands and generating employment and income for women. Women donated wasteland they owned to a women's society and planted mulberry trees thus contributing to women's employment and income generation, in addition to regenerating wastelands. Following the success of this experiment, neighboring villages and other women's societies have successfully reclaimed lands laid waste through systematic deforestation. Much of the experiment's success was a result of women's own initiative, entrepreneurship, and ability to organize and manage their enterprises collectively, supplemented by technical and financial support from the state government and NGOs.
- In India, the Chipko movement, in which women literally "hugged" the trees to prevent commercial tree felling, attracted state government attention. The result was an investigation that led to a ten-year ban on tree felling in that area.

Source: Mehra and others 1992.

---

and lowers the administrative costs per loan, which is particularly important if the average loan is very small. The groups take over many of the screening, incentive, and enforcement functions normally left to banking staff. Group lending also spares borrowers elaborate application procedures, transportation costs, and the need for collateral. Other techniques for lowering transaction costs include inexpensive and mobile offices, hiring of staff from client communities, and standardized and decentralized procedures for lending.

Group lending also lowers the risk of default. The combination of peer pressure and cooperative gains from participation in a group has proved to be an effective motivator for repayment in many different countries and settings worldwide. The Grameen Bank's loan recovery rates exceed 98 percent. The twenty-seven organizations affiliated with the ACCION network (an NGO for microenterprise lending) in Latin America and the Caribbean have an average 96–97 percent repayment rate, far higher than the national averages for commercial banks. The risk of default to the overall viability of the lending institution is also minimized by the common practice of making small, short-term loans, and by rewarding good repayment performance with repeat loans of escalating value. The average loan size at the Grameen Bank is well under $100.

Box 6. Principles of Financially Viable Lending to Poor Entrepeneurs

Principle 1: Offer services that fit the preferences of poor entrepreneurs

- Offer short loan terms, compatible with enterprise outlay and income patterns. ACCION programs and BKK typically lend for three-month terms; the Grameen family of programs, for one year.
- Offer repeat loans. Full repayment of one loan brings access to another. Repeat lending allows credit to support financial management as a process, not an isolated event.
- Allow relatively unrestricted use of loan. While most programs select customers with active enterprises (and thus cash flow for repayment), there are few limitations on the uses of loans. Thus, clients have decisionmaking flexibility to use funds for household or enterprise purposes.
- Extend very small loans, appropriate for meeting the day-to-day financial requirements of women's businesses. Average loan sizes at BKK and Grameen are well under $100, while most ACCION programs and BRI feature average loans in the $200 to $800 range.
- Make operations customer friendly (low client transaction costs). Locate outlets close to entrepreneurs; use extremely simple applications (often one page), and limit time between application and disbursement to a few days. Develop a public image of being approachable by poor people.

Principle 2: Streamline operations to reduce unit costs

- Develop highly streamlined operations, minimizing staff time per loan. Standardize the lending process. Application contents should be very simple and be evaluated on the basis of easily verifiable criteria. Loan approvals should be decentralized. Operational costs

---

Lack of collateral is a pervasive problem for the poor, and particularly for poor women, who rarely have title to significant assets. Joint-liability groups replace collateral with a collective guarantee in many programs. Other institutions, such as Indonesia's Badan Kredit Kecamatan (BKK), make initial loans on the basis of character references from local officials—another method of mobilizing peer pressure. Many institutions that provide credit to the poor also have compulsory savings schemes as part of their programs. The Grameen Bank requires that 5 percent of the amount of each loan be deposited in a group fund and encourages other savings in emergency funds, and children's welfare funds.

should be reduced as BKK does, by operating its village posts once a week from rooms in local government buildings, paying little or no overhead while reaching deep into rural areas. Staff may be selected from local communities, including people with lower levels of education (and hence salaries) than staff in formal banking institutions.

Principle 3: Motivate clients to repay loans

- Substitute for preloan project analysis and formal collateral by assuming that clients will be *able* to repay. Concentrate on providing *motivation* to repay.
- Joint-liability groups, where a handful of borrowers guarantee each others' loans, are by far the most frequently used repayment motivator, employed by Grameen and in slightly different form by ACCION affiliates. This technique had proved effective in many different countries and settings worldwide. Individual character lending can be effective where the social structure is cohesive, as has been demonstrated throughout Indonesia's array of credit programs.
- Incentives, such as guaranteeing access to loans, increasing loan sizes, and preferential pricing all for prompt repayers, should be offered. Institutions that successfully motivate repayments also develop staff competence and a public image signaling that they are serious about loan collection.

Principle 4: Charge full-cost interest rates and fees

- The small loan sizes necessary to serve the poor still result in costs per loan which require interest rates that may be significantly higher than commercial bank rates (although significantly lower than informal sector rates). However, poor entrepreneurs have shown willingness and ability to pay such rates for services with attributes that fit their needs.

Source: Rhyne and Holt 1993.

In some settings, institutions offering credit and savings services to poor women have encountered uncooperativeness and even opposition from influential members of participants' families. To overcome this, the Grameen Bank, with its 94 percent female membership, has instituted a series of family workshops for the husbands, brothers, fathers, and sons of bank members. The workshops explain the philosophy and objectives of the bank to encourage effective use of the loans and other services it provides. This can help diffuse misunderstandings among participants' relatives and motivate them to cooperate with the members.

Providing access to financial services is necessary but not sufficient. People who have never used a bank must be taught how to do so. Training and confidence-building are especially important for women, who are likely to have less formal education and less experience with formal organizations and procedures. Alongside financial services, it is imperative to equip women with training in small enterprise, entrepreneurship, and management—how to begin and successfully sustain an enterprise. Thus, peer support, mentoring, and training are crucial to the success of programs that reach out to those previously underserved. The Grameen Bank fosters attitudinal change by promoting behavior and values it feels are conducive to better lives for its members— opposing dowry payments, for example, and promoting hygiene and education. The program has been replicated in many countries. The Bank has also contributed to the Grameen Trust, which will help advance this type of program in other developing countries.

5

The Roles of Governments and
the World Bank

Public policy can significantly enhance women's participation in economic development. In some instances, the contribution may consist largely of training and supporting the activities of nongovernmental agencies, communities, and parents. In others, it may take the form of changing the legal and institutional frameworks. However, tangible progress depends on the active involvement, leadership, and commitment of governments.

The World Bank will support member governments in implementing the operational strategies outlined in the previous chapter. Its economic and sector work, lending, technical assistance, and participation in international initiatives will aim at promoting gender-sensitive policies and programs. To do this, the Bank will help address the legal and regulatory frameworks that prevent women from participating in economic development, strengthen institutional capacity in the member countries to implement programs for advancing women's status in the five areas reviewed in Chapter 4, and mobilize international resources to help reduce gender disparities. The Bank does not intend to limit the activities on gender to these five areas. However, the implementation experience of integrating gender issues within and outside the Bank in other areas has only begun to emerge; by contrast, these five areas offer immediate and unambiguous strategies. The Bank will continue to advance the knowledge on gender issues, promote gender-sensitive policies and programs in *all* areas through an analysis of the implications of gender disparities, and derive best practices for addressing them.

Strengthening the Data Base for Gender Analysis

In all countries, public agencies are responsible for collecting and publishing the data used to monitor progress toward economic and social objectives. Surprisingly few developing countries systematically gather and report statistics disaggregated by gender. In the absence of such information, even marked disparities may go unrecognized. The ability of governments to identify areas of concern, to design appropriate remedial action, and to monitor progress depends on the availability of gender-disaggregated data. Government action in this area is straightforward: to ensure that basic socioeconomic statistics (school enrollments, life expectancy at birth, mortality, labor force participation, and so forth) are recorded separately for men and women. Similarly, information on the outcomes of specific programs should be gender specific. It is absolutely essential to collect baseline data whenever a new program or project is being launched so that the effectiveness of interventions can be rigorously assessed.

The Bank will support the collection and analysis of gender-disaggregated data in its borrowing countries through its technical assistance in the design and analysis of household data sets such as the Living Standard Measurement Surveys. In countries with well-established statistical bureaus and data collection instruments, it may be possible to ensure that most data collected are reported by gender. In countries where data-gathering capacity is more limited, a first step may be to report basic socioeconomic data by gender. The Bank is in a position to organize appropriate financial and technical assistance to support these efforts.

Developing Gender-Sensitive Policies and Programs

The Bank can assist governments in identifying gender issues through a variety of instruments, from country economic memoranda and public expenditure reviews to poverty assessments, analytical reports on gender issues, and sector reports (for example, in education, health, and agriculture). Whatever the vehicle, the objective should be to develop a clear understanding of the current status of women's (or girls') access to services and productive assets, the current policies affecting access, and key issues for the Bank's dialogue with the country. An example of such analysis is the country economic memorandum on Uganda (Box 7).

The Bank can assist governments wishing to reduce gender disparities in going beyond gender-neutral public policies to ensure that the *outcomes* of policy are equally beneficial to men and women. For example, governments in many countries have taken measures to expand educational enrollments at all levels but have found that specific initiatives are needed to overcome the barriers to girls' attendance so that enrollment, attainment, and quality outcomes are gender neutral. In some cases, such changes may involve attitudinal changes as in China (Box 8). The Bank will support governments in formulating policies and in designing public programs for increasing girls' enrollment. In other cases, such changes will have a significant impact on the education budget—as is the case for scholarships to girls, for example, which normally involve additional costs. In such cases, the Bank will assist the governments in assessing program costs and benefits, both economic and social (including the intergenerational effects). If significant additional resources are justified, the Bank could assist in mobilizing international resources to help implement the program.

Modifying the Legal and Regulatory Framework

Governments have the capacity to remove barriers to women's control over productive assets and resources by modifying legal and regulatory frameworks. Many governments—facing demands on time and resources—have not paid enough attention to laws and regulations that limit women's options and reinforce their economic disadvantage. Even where laws are gender neutral on paper, the application and enforcement by the courts can be discriminatory. Allowing women to own land can improve their access to inputs and credit that raise their productivity, and removing legal barriers can open segments of the formal labor market once closed to women. Social and cultural barriers to opportunity may remain, but an important first step for any government is to confirm unequivocally its intent to ensure equal legal access to jobs, assets, and services. The next step is to make the appropriate changes in laws and regulations. The final step is to ensure that the institutional measures are in place to implement the legal changes.

In many countries, the constitutional provisions for the equality of the sexes already exist. Needed, however, is the translation of these provisions into reality through changes in legislation and regulations. Where appropriate and feasible, the Bank will assist governments in their efforts to reform and establish a strong legal and regulatory framework in order to tackle the access problems for women and improve their productivity. Similarly, the Bank will support institutional measures at national and local levels to implement changes in the legal and regulatory framework.

Ensuring Effective Program Delivery

Well-designed policies and programs are not enough—they need to be effectively implemented. Governments need to pursue complementary

---

Box 7. Analyzing Gender Issues in the World Bank's Country Economic Memoranda: An Illustration from Uganda

Within the context of an overall strategy for labor-intensive growth and human resource development, the report focuses on the gender dimensions of poverty. The analysis adopts the view that poverty affects men and women in different ways because they play different roles, have different needs, and face different constraints in responding to policy changes and to shifts in incentives. This combination of differences arises from fundamental imbalances in the respective rights and obligations of men and women and translates into their having very different economic capacities, as reflected in their access to, use of, and control over economically productive resources. These differences have implications not only for economic equity but also for economic efficiency and forgone output and income.

The poverty profile is presented with particular emphasis on gender. Identification of the poor and vulnerable groups includes discussions on female-headed households and disabled, widowed, and divorced women. In addition, the predominance of intrahousehold inequality, whereby mothers and daughters have to wait until fathers and older sons are fed before they can eat, is pointed out as a major factor contributing to the poor nutritional status of women. This has serious implications for maternal and child mortality, low-birth-weight babies, and problematic lactation.

An interesting footnote is that the survey and census data used to construct the poverty profile was supplemented by results from a Rapid Poverty Appraisal by Bank staff. These participatory rural appraisals solicited opinions from the rural poor as to how they view poverty and its causes. Even small children who cannot yet write were asked to draw pictures of the poor.

The report illustrates the relevance of gender in assessing poverty and stressing the importance of incorporating gender concerns into the formulation and design of strategies for reducing poverty and promoting economic growth. The most pressing issues with respect to women's multiple roles and constraints, in relation to those of men, are identified as the basis for the Bank's recommendations for raising the status and productivity of women; women lack technology, inputs, and finance to

---

strategies to make sure that programs reach women. Programs to promote contraception are more effective when combined with female education and with programs of income generation for women. And programs to encourage female schooling beyond the secondary level can be combined with skill training programs related to labor market decarry out their agricultural tasks. They hold multiple household responsibilities without the benefit of labor-saving technology or adequate social service and transport infrastructure—a heavy workload without due compensation. Low health and nutritional status constrain women's capacity to provide for the health of other family members and limit economic productivity and potential. Low levels of literacy and increasing gender inequity at different levels of education compound the difficulties faced by women in meeting their many responsibilities. Laws and customs impede women to a greater extent than men in obtaining credit, productive inputs, education, training, information, and medical care. And gender division of labor causes women to remain in the unpaid subsistence sector.

Given the competing claims on women's time, linkages between poverty, lack of access to and control of economic resources, and survival strategies have particular importance. Related issues include the interdependence of economically productive and social sector investments and programs, the socioeconomic implications of AIDS for household survival strategies, poverty reduction and economic prospects, and the problem of low female participation in education.

In response to these problems, the Ugandan government has adopted gender-responsive actions that will be undertaken as an interconnected package of mutually reinforcing measures . They include the support of legal reforms and the promotion of legal rights and protections that enable women to benefit from their own labor and to have greater access to and control of economically productive resources, thereby raising their status. Programs to raise the productivity of women's economic (paid) labor through investment in education are aimed at overcoming social, financial, and cultural barriers to female participation through investment in basic, accessible, and affordable health care and through targeted actions aimed at raising women's access to information, technology, inputs, credit, and extension services. Measures to alleviate the domestic labor constraint include investments in labor-saving technologies, infrastructure, water supply, and woodlots that take explicit account of female users' needs in design and implementation. Finally, efforts spearheaded by UNICEF to reduce AIDS risk among young girls will receive maximum political and financial support.

mands. More attention to program monitoring and evaluation will help, by signaling both successes and failures in reaching women.

Staff training is critical for building the awareness and strengthening the capacity of line officials who deal with the needs of disadvantaged women. Involving women directly in project design can make program

---

Box 8. How Government Policy Can Ensure Gender-Neutral Outcomes: China's Experience in Raising Primary Enrollments

In China, several provinces introduced compulsory education laws prior to the nine-year compulsory education law of 1986. Important follow-up efforts by the government included decentralization of responsibility for primary education and introduction of cost reduction strategies via community efforts. Policy measures to raise primary enrollments, especially of girls, have been devised at the local level. This allowed regional differences in constraints to be reflected in ameliorative policies. The programs have included awareness campaigns to motivate parents to enroll all children (enlisting religious leaders and the Women's Federation in the effort); active community support; a responsibility system whereby principals and teachers were encouraged to enroll and retain students; the opening of alternative channels, including flexible schedules, night classes, and programs combining work and study; provision of sibling care; modest financial assistance (waiving tuition and providing monthly stipends); and special schools for girls. These measures involved close government interaction with the communities and parents. The program raised girls' (as well as boys') enrollments even in the poor rural and mountainous regions, enabling China to nearly reach the goal of universal primary education despite its low per capita income.

Sources: Coletta and Sutton 1989; Herz and others 1991.

---

delivery more effective. Recruiting women for service delivery positions often attracts more women to use them, thereby increasing program effectiveness. Flexible program delivery can also be very helpful. Even simple changes towards flexibility can have profound outcomes. For example, in India the delivery of nutrition supplements to pregnant landless farm women was greatly improved by offering the supplements on a flexible schedule that did not take women away from the fields during working hours. In agrarian settings, flexible school hours and school calendars are important for attracting girls to schools.

Working with NGOs can often improve program effectiveness because NGOS can adapt more readily to changes in local needs and requirements (Box 9). NGOS may also be better placed to mobilize local participation in the planning, design, implementation, and management of projects, especially if they have local roots and an understanding of behaviors and practices at the community level. Governments can promote participation by adopting policies supportive of NGOS' initiatives, by listening to women's representatives, and by encouraging political participation of

---

Box 9. Involving Women's Organizations in Project Implementation: The Role of the *Mahila Samakhya* Program in the Uttar Pradesh Basic Education Project in India

The Uttar Pradesh Basic Education Project is intended to permit an additional 1 million students to complete their education and to provide 600,000 students who are currently unserved with access to basic education services. The project has three components: building institutional capacity, improving the quality and completion of primary education in ten districts, and improving access by constructing additional facilities.

To ensure community support and the full participation of women in its orientation and implementation, the *Mahila Samakhya* (MS) women's empowerment program has been built into the project design. MS, which is an autonomous body, has extensive experience in creating and working with village women's groups that are a forum for discussion and action on problems confronting village women. Key principles of the MS program include the following:

- Project functionaries and officials are facilitative and not directive.
- Planning, decisionmaking, and evaluative processes are accountable to the collective of village women.
- Women participants determine the form, nature, content, and timing of all activities in their village and that staff selection processes are participatory.
- The program is not hurried and does not have targets but is a self-paced process built on existing knowledge and women's own priorities for learning.

At the district level, the MS structure will interact in a structured way with the district education machinery to coordinate program implementation. At the state level, the MS State Project Director will be a member of the General Council and the Executive Committee of the EFA (Education For All) Society.

The role of MS will gradually be expanded as the project evolves. It will be involved in vitalizing the project, assisting with staffing, and helping with expansion. MS will sensitize the district-level development and education personnel in each new group of villages that is integrated into the project.

---

women in decisionmaking. Involving women at every level of program planning, design, and implementation is virtually a prerequisite for success.

To support governments' endeavors to ensure success in program delivery, the Bank will identify gender-related roles, interests, and constraints to ensure that the multiple barriers that women face relative to those of men are addressed in early project and program design. Where appropriate, the Bank will promote a package approach to address these barriers (Box 10). Its international experience can also help in identifying

---

Box 10. The World Bank's Experience with the "Package Approach"

To minimize the gender gap and enhance girls' enrollments, many Bank-assisted projects, both new and continuing, employ a "package approach" (incorporating multiple interventions). Although it is too early to evaluate these projects, they indicate the potential for integrated approaches and practices.

Bangladesh General Education Project. This project addresses in-school, out-of-school, and sociocultural barriers simultaneously to raise female participation in primary and secondary schools. To increase girls' access to schooling, in addition to regular primary schools, 2001 nonformal primary schools have been opened with the help of NGOs, and 200 pilot satellite schools have been built closer to girls' homes. All the teachers in both the nonformal and the satellite schools are female. These schools also offer the flexible schedules, set in consultation with village committees, appropriate for rural areas. Teachers work closely with mothers to motivate girls' to attend schools. A new feature is the provision of childcare for younger siblings at the schools. The Female Secondary Scholarship Program, which decreased dropout rates and improved attendance rates even for girls not receiving scholarships, is being continued. To make government schools attractive to girls, experimental programs including school feeding, provision of uniforms, and community outreach programs are to be introduced. A WID cell has been established within the national Curriculum and Textbooks Board that examines girls' learning needs and develops motivational materials in the form of comics and cartoons for girls. New curricula with gender messages are introduced in primary schools. The provision for hiring 60 percent of all new female primary school teachers is to be increased in the Primary Teachers Training Institutions (PTIS). The project also provides improved teacher training facilities for women and aims at reducing gender bias in teaching methods and attitudes. To attract female students in PTIS, dormitory facilities that include study area, latrine, and washing facilities have been provided. Gender stereotypes are to be removed from textbooks and other teaching materials. In addition, curriculum content is to include such issues as gender roles and responsibilities and the status of women. A WID monitoring guideline has been developed for continuous supervision, monitoring, and evaluations. Because of these concerted interventions, as the preliminary results show, girls' enrollments

successful strategies that can be applied to a particular situation. The Bank will also assist governments in establishing monitoring mechanisms either at the national level or at the project level to evaluate the effectiveness of program delivery in various interventions. Identifying

---

at the primary level increased from 45 percent in 1990 to 54 percent in 1993. More girls than boys attend satellite schools. Retention rates have also increased at the primary level.

Bangladesh Female Secondary Schools Assistance Project. This project offers an integrated package approach to address both direct and opportunity costs of secondary school girls. The Female Education Scholarship Program is the basic model for the Female Secondary School Assistance Program (FSSAP). The model is being adapted by structuring stipend rates to reflect rising educational costs from lower to upper grades and to provide extra incentives for reducing high dropout rates in upper grades. Apart from stipends to girls, the project incorporates a number of other measures to respond to the severe barriers girls face in Bangladesh. The goals of these measures are to (a) increase the proportion of female teachers; (b) provide occupational skills related to market demand and suitable for wage employment or self-employment, including job counseling and placement; (c) promote public support for girls education through a widespread community awareness program regarding the social and economic benefits of female education; (d) provide a healthier and safer setting for girls and increase attractiveness of schools through community participation in school-based water supply and sanitation programs; and (e) to strengthen the implementation capacity for the project at the national and local levels, through, among other means, a management information monitoring and evaluation system. This package approach will help close the gender gap in access to secondary education, increase the proportion of female graduates, and decrease the average number of years of schooling it takes to produce one female graduate. It will also instill a sense of confidence among girls through increased mobility around the community and interaction with the banking system and increase the girls' access to productive work.

The example of projects in Bangladesh is particularly interesting, as it shows that in very poor countries, the package approach and follow-up projects can have a lasting impact on girls' education. A number of other countries, including the Gambia, Morocco, and Pakistan, use the package approach to address distance, financial, and cultural constraints on female education.

Source: Herz and others 1991; Chowdhury 1993.

roles, as well as monitoring program effectiveness, entails gathering gender-disaggregated data.

In tandem with improving the design of programs addressing gender issues, the Bank will support the training of country policymakers, planners, project managers, and technicians in gender analysis. Training may be integrated into courses provided by the Bank in various areas or may be provided through self-standing seminars on women and gender issues. The Bank will also endeavor to leverage its resources by training trainers in selected countries in gender analysis. These trainers can then adapt the training to their particular environment.

Mobilizing Resources

The resource implications of a program for enhancing women's contribution to economic development in a given country depends in large part on the past investments in human resource development. In countries where investments have been limited, access and quality of services will be low for men and women. In such cases, efforts to reduce gender disparities are unlikely to have significant resource implications of their own, although some resources will need to be diverted to improve program design and delivery to women within the broader framework of efforts to increase investments in human resource development. In most cases, program and policy changes do not involve additional costs. Resource implications may actually be greater in countries where investments in human resource development have been substantial but where gender disparities are also large. These countries will face difficult decisions on whether to reallocate resources from one group to another or find additional resources to expand services to the underserved group. Because decisions to reallocate funds are often politically unpopular, governments may decide to extend services only when they can mobilize additional resources. The Bank will assist countries by ensuring that its own lending in these sectors supports the expansion of women's access. It can also help to mobilize additional international resources by emphasizing bilateral cofinancing for its operations, organizing consultative group meetings for assisting specific countries, and supporting any resource mobilization initiatives targeted to expanding investments in women that may emerge from the 1995 Fourth World Conference on Women in Beijing.

Implications for World Bank Operations

Analyzing issues and experience. The barriers and approaches described in this policy paper are intended to highlight key issues and strategies for enhancing women's contribution to economic development based on accumulated evidence over the last two decades. They are not prescribed solutions for all country environments. The issues vary from one country to another. Thus, as a first step, the analysis of gender issues should be carried out for each country to identify the issues and to apply relevant lessons of experience through a variety of instruments. In most cases, the best diagnostic instrument will be the country poverty assessments, which are expected to analyze social indicators by gender and give substantial attention to the key sectors discussed above. In most countries, there is significant overlap between gender issues and poverty issues.

Integrating gender issues into country assistance strategies. The formulation of a country assistance strategy is one of the Bank's principal vehicles for policy dialogues with governments. Accordingly, the second step is to integrate these issues into country strategy papers where appropriate. In integrating gender concerns into country assistance strategies, the Bank will need to assess governments' own positions and constraints, especially those associated with cultural norms and deep-seated traditions. This does not mean that country strategies should take traditional biases as immutable; it does mean that assessments and targets will need to be realistic in order to achieve meaningful dialogues and results. The most effective way to develop consensus around such strategies for improving gender equity may be to set specific objectives for sectors in which gender disparities are particularly acute and demonstrably costly. Specific objectives might include establishing a five-year target for expanding girls' enrollments in primary school, expanding the network of family planning and reproductive health services, increasing women farmers' access to productive inputs, and making enterprise development services and credit programs more available to women.

Country dialogue on gender should have the highest priority in countries and sectors where the problems of gender inequity are most acute. This is not meant to discourage Bank staff from working in every country to achieve greater gender equality. However, a focused strategy can help ensure that attention is systematically paid to those key countries and sectors where underinvestment in women has been most serious. The countries where gender inequity is greatest may be precisely where progress may be most difficult, because of deeply held cultural norms. This does not invalidate the proposed approach. It does mean that country gender strategies need to be realistic in expectations and grounded in a careful assessment of social, cultural, and political factors.

Designing and implementing a lending program. The third step in the Bank's strategy is the design and implementation of a lending program that supports the achievement of tangible progress in closing the gender gap through both adjustment and investment operations, where appropriate. Both the types of operations in the lending program and the design of those operations should be congruent with the objective of reducing gender disparities in a specific way. For example, in a country in which the primary education enrollment ratio for girls is less than 40 percent for the age group, a specific goal might be to increase this to 50 percent over a specified period, and the Bank's lending program would correspondingly include basic education projects to support this goal. In most cases, the achievement of specific sectoral goals will require attention to sectoral policies, the legal framework, institutional capacity, and other social and cultural issues in order to identify the full range of constraints.

During project design, the focus is not to promote women's activities in isolation but to find ways and means of enhancing women's participation in a given sector and to link the activities of men and women more effectively within the project with a view to ensuring optimum overall project benefits. It is necessary, therefore, to identify at an early stage gender-related roles, interests, and constraints, to clarify project objectives, and to define operational means (both institutional and financial) that facilitate women's access to project activities, benefits, and facilities. For example, if poverty reduction is an objective, and if women are primary and secondary income earners, analysis is needed of their economic activities and of the constraints on their participation, which are normally different from those of men. Specific components—policy reforms, institutional measures, or financial incentives, depending on local conditions—could then be designed to remove or circumvent the barriers (Box 11).

Projects should also include performance indicators to measure progress, as well as monitoring and evaluation mechanisms to follow up on implementation. Because gender issues have important local, social, and cultural dimensions, Bank staff may need to call on NGOs, academics, local consultants, and other donors with experience in gender issues for support in this work.

Although the Bank's strategy is to mainstream gender issues in projects as a matter of course, it also recognizes that in some country environments, self-standing women-in-development projects may be necessary to pioneer efforts to promote women's participation in development. It is important, however, that these activities be integrated into existing institutions in the long run to ensure their sustainability, or the design should be such that beneficiaries themselves can carry on activities without relying on external support.

Adjustment policies encompassing macroeconomic stabilization, public expenditure reform, public enterprise restructuring, and trade

Box 11. The Gender Analysis Framework

The gender analysis framework distinguishes between sex and gender, acknowledging that while biological differences have provided the base, gender characteristics, activities, and roles have been shaped over time by sociocultural and economic factors. Since gender (the social differentiation between women and men in a particular context) is socially and culturally constructed, gender roles can be transformed by social changes, induced by economic transformation, incentives, and legal and regulatory reforms.

Gender analysis is the practical tool for analyzing the nature of gender differentiation. It builds information by asking questions about who does what, where, when, and with what resources, in order to determine the structure of gender activity, including time use, as well as the nature of resource ownership, use, and control.

Carried out systematically, gender analysis should provide adequate knowledge regarding the major factors that influence and are responsible for maintaining or changing the structure of gender differentiation. With this knowledge, appropriate policy or interventions can be designed to help enhance women's status and productivity.

For example, in most rural low-income households in developing countries, the primary role of men is to earn income. Women, in contrast, have a triple role: they are responsible for reproductive work (childbearing, child-rearing, and household welfare activities); for productive work (crop planting and processing, livestock raising, handicrafts, and so on) and for community managing (the provision and maintenance of community services such as healthcare, nutrition, and water supply).

Understanding these roles in a specific context would imply that an agricultural extension program needs to be designed around women's schedules and meeting places to elicit their participation, as they have to balance these three roles. Male farmers can adapt to fixed schedules and meeting places, since they are mainly involved in income earning activities.

As mentioned in chapter 4, in many developing countries, women's businesses (as compared to men's) are smaller and slower growing, essentially as a result of women's need to perform socially and culturally defined roles. Using gender analysis in this case would help to shape the type of financial services that would best serve women—such as small and repeatable loans and simple loan processing—without resorting to targeting and interest subsidy.

Source: Moser 1993; Rhyne and Holt 1993.

policy reform may all have adverse short-term impacts on the population. In some countries and situations, such short-term adverse effects may fall disproportionately on women. Two examples illustrate the issue. First, some policies may result in job losses and women may suffer job losses disproportionately, as is the case in Eastern Europe and the FSU. Second, because women and men may differ in the consumption of public services (for example, health clinics and piped water), budgetary contraction can have gender-differentiated effects.

Adjustment policies do set in motion beneficial changes in the economy. However, the beneficial effects of adjustment policies may be slow in reaching women. The analysis in previous chapters has shown that women face different constraints from men. Adjustment policies typically remove price distortions and restore profitability of certain crops and activities, but women may not be able to take advantage of such beneficial changes unless their particular constraints are removed. For example, some crops may become profitable following the removal of price distortions, but women, constrained by inadequate family labor supply or credit or other resources, may not participate in such profitable activities.

Thus, adjustment policies can have adverse short-term impacts, these adverse effects may be more pronounced on women than on men, and women may not always benefit immediately from favorable policy changes. In designing adjustment operations, it is important to recognize the differential adverse short-term impacts of adjustment policies. To the extent that the impacts can be identified, the Bank will need to incorporate safety net measures in the adjustment program. Where data are inadequate for assessing the differential impacts by gender of adjustment policies, the Bank will need to help the government generate gender-disaggregated data. At the same time, the Bank will continue to work with governments through appropriate channels to remove the particular barriers faced by women so that they too can benefit from the favorable effects of adjustment policies.

Advancing knowledge on gender and development. The Bank will help support developing countries' efforts to enhance women's economic contributions in another important way. The Bank's ongoing program of policy-oriented work will continue to analyze the economic implications of gender disparities and the particular issues in transitional economies and identify operational best practices for addressing them. The Bank's international perspective enables it to draw on experiences in many countries to distill information about policy impact and best practices and guide the policies and programs of national governments and other donors, in addition to the Bank's own operations. Recent Bank-funded research on credit schemes in Bangladesh is an example of work that examines the effects of program design and implementation on the productivity and welfare of women, with important implications for policy.

Much of the proposed policy analysis has a direct bearing on the nature of gender differentiation and the factors influencing the structure of gender relations within households. The traditional neoclassical analysis assumes that household behavior reflects the preferences of all its individuals, so that public policies and projects reach individuals unhampered by household behavior. Gender analysis, on the other hand, postulates that (a) a web of social relationships characterizes every household; (b) there are differences in preferences among household members that are resolved through a bargaining process; and, therefore, (c) the policies and projects that filter through the household may affect men and women differentially.

Specific priorities for future Bank analysis include investigating how patterns of intrafamily resource allocation can reduce or enhance the effects of public policy and what incentive systems can be used to stimulate changes in social, cultural, and legal institutions that limit the activities and rights of women relative to men. Studies will also explore the association between low investments in women and a higher incidence of death and illness among girls and women (whether because of domestic violence, neglect, maternal mortality, disease—including AIDS, or other causes); the possibility that adjustment policies have different impacts on men and women; the legal and regulatory barriers that prevent women from participating in economic activities; and the positive impact that women's participation in natural resources management can have on the environment. Finally, future analysis will also document examples of the costly and unintended adverse effects on women's welfare stemming from the neglect of the analysis of gender roles and intrahousehold bargaining processes. The availability of large-scale household data sets such as the Bank's Living Standards Measurement Surveys will facilitate quick completion of such policy analysis.

The Bank will also build knowledge by supporting pilot schemes to identify best practices in areas where the payoffs could be great. Not enough is yet known about what works. Pilot programs provide an opportunity to test delivery mechanisms and incentive schemes and to bring about institutional and attitudinal changes. Pilot schemes have already been used successfully, for example, in the development of a Bank-supported agricultural project in Côte d'Ivoire. In Chile, a Bank-supported grant is assisting an integrated pilot program addressing issues as diverse as domestic violence, childcare, and skills training.

Monitoring and evaluation. The Bank will also strengthen its current monitoring system to assess the progress in integrating gender in the Bank's operations. The system will monitor the gender analysis carried out in economic and sector work and the linkage to the Bank's lending operations. Evaluation of implementation efforts "on the ground" will also be carried out as a part of country implementation reviews to the

Bank's Board of Executive Directors. Progress in implementing the recommended policy will be reported to the Board periodically.

Implementation. Implementation of the above strategy will require special efforts in three areas: gender assessments, the development of pilot programs, and impact evaluations, to build up our knowledge about effective approaches. These areas have implications for the Bank in terms of resources and staff skills mix. Diagnostic analyses of gender issues may require (a) gathering information from nontraditional sources, and in some cases, generating primary data; and (b) some specialist skills (such as microenterprise development specialists and social scientists) that may not be sufficiently available in the Bank. Impact evaluations to measure progress and effectiveness can be costly to design and carry out and may also require expertise that may not be sufficiently available in the Bank.

These costs to the country departments will vary from one country to another, depending on the availability of information and the commitment of governments to addressing gender issues. It is likely that in countries where acute gender disparities exist, operationalization of the strategy will imply significant resource reallocations within a specific country work program, within a country department, or even across country departments or regions. By collaborating with other donors and leveraging agencies' resources and expertise, it may be possible to reduce these costs somewhat. But implementation of the strategy will not be resource neutral. The Human Resources Development and Operations Policy Vice Presidency, in collaboration with country departments, is working on "mainstreaming" gender issues in order to draw lessons of experience for the Bank in terms of budgetary and skills-mix implications.

To improve staff skills, an intensive training program will be put in place to create an awareness of the importance of addressing gender issues in Bank operations and to provide tools and practical knowledge for policy and project design in various areas. In addition to the dissemination of important analytical results, the Bank will also disseminate operational tool kits that will help Bank staff discuss "what to do" and "what works" with governments in various country environments.

Learning from and collaborating with others. Other bilateral and multilateral donors and NGOs have extensive experience dealing with gender issues—in many cases, more than the Bank has. Studies assessing the experience of the member countries of the OECD's Development Assistance Committee (DAC) in formulating and implementing women in development policies during the last decade have just been completed.[3] These studies, undertaken by the Expert Group on Women in Development and Aid Evaluation, have assisted in identifying areas of progress and effective strategies and instruments, as well as in highlighting important gaps between intentions and results. A similar study for United Nations organizations is now being prepared. The 1995 Fourth World Conference on Women provides an opportunity for various agencies to examine and better coordinate their past and present women in development policies.

All the studies point out that substantial progress has been made in institutionalizing women's concerns and in supporting action in DAC donor organizations. Gender issues are gaining visibility in donor agency documents, and sectoral and cross-cutting themes have increasingly addressed gender concerns. Progress is measured in terms of the increase in the number of projects by assistance organizations that include women in development components in donor organizations, the increase in resources for women-in-development initiatives, and the improved awareness and expertise of staff regarding gender issues.

However, gaps still remain. At the donor level, there are still obstacles to the implementation of gender policies. They include inadequate accountability measures within institutions for addressing gender concerns, a lack of clear indicators for monitoring progress, and persistent gaps in awareness of and expertise in handling gender issues in donor organizations. At the recipient country level, the implementation of women-in-development measures appears modest, at times even marginal. Moreover, most governments and donors have not yet established quantitative and qualitative measures by which to track the impact and effectiveness of women-in-development policies and measures.

Many donors advocate a strategy that is built on a partnership between donor and recipient country and development of a common understanding of issues, priorities, and approaches if gender disparities are to be reduced. The Bank will collaborate in this effort by (a) assisting member countries to develop the institutional capacity to formulate national policies—as in the case of the grants the Institutional Development Fund awarded Chile and Iran; (b) building a wide-ranging consultation process with governments, NGOs, and multilateral and bilateral donors on gender issues in specific country environments in order to ensure the relevance of the Bank's country assistance strategy on gender concerns; (c) enhancing awareness and expertise by using local capacities in generating data, conducting surveys, and analyzing results; and (d) increasing the participation of women in the decisionmaking phases of development program and project design.

It is important to recognize the comparative advantage of various players in integrating gender concerns into the development agenda. While some organizations can have more impact on ensuring that gender concerns are part of the political process in partner countries, the

Bank can contribute best by focusing its efforts on generating analytical knowledge by ensuring that its own country-specific economic policies and projects are gender sensitive and responsive and by helping national (government and nongovernment) organizations to develop and implement their own agendas for closing the gender gap, through emphasis on participation and ownership that includes both women and men.

Finally, it bears repeating that the efforts of donors, NGOs, and the international agencies will bear fruit only with governments' leadership, commitment, and collaboration.

Endnotes

1. For details on the distinction, see Moser (1993).

2. Private economic rate of return is defined as the rate that equates the costs to the study with the present discounted value of the increase in net income (less taxes) that the student will earn with an education. For details on the definition and method for estimation, see Schultz (1993).

3. These include Australia, Belgium, Canada, Denmark, France, Germany, Ireland, Italy, Japan, the Netherlands, Norway, Portugal, Sweden, Switzerland, the United Kingdom, and the United States.

Bibliography

Acharya, Meena, and Lynn Bennett. 1983. "Women and the Subsistence Sector: Economic Participation and Household Decision-Making in Nepal." World Bank Working Paper 526. Washington, D.C.

Anker, Richard, and Catherine Hein. 1986. *Sex Inequalities in Urban Employment in the Third World*. New York: St. Martin's Press.

Appleton, Simon, and others. 1991. *Public Services and Household Allocation in Africa: Does Gender Matter?* Oxford, U.K.: Oxford University, Center for African Studies.

Bach, Rebecca, and Saad Gadalla. 1985. "Mothers' Influence on Daughters' Orientations Toward Education: An Egyptian Case Study." *Comparative Education Review* 29:374–84.

Bellew, Rosemary, and E. King. 1993. "Educating Women: Lessons from Experience." In Elizabeth King and Ann Hill, eds., *Women's Education in Developing Countries: Barriers, Benefits, and Policies*. Baltimore, Md.: Johns Hopkins University Press.

Birdsall, Nancy. 1993. *Social Development is Economic Development*. Washington, D.C.: The World Bank.

Chatterjee, Meera. 1991. *Indian Women: Their Health and Economic Productivity*. World Bank Discussion Paper 109. Washington, D.C.

Chowdhury, K. 1993. "Women in Education." World Bank, Education and Social Policy Department, Washington, D.C.

Coletta, Nat J., and Margaret Sutton. 1989. "Achieving and Sustaining Universal Primary Education: International Experience Relevant to India." Policy, Research, and External Affairs Working Paper 166. World Bank, Population and Human Resources Department, Washington, D.C.

El-Sanabary, Nagat. 1993. "Middle East and Northern Africa." In *Women's Education in Developing Countries*. Baltimore, Md.: Johns Hopkins University Press.

Fong, Monica S. 1992. *The Role of Women in Rebuilding the Russian Economy*. Studies of Economies in Transformation Paper 10. Washington, D.C.: World Bank.

Fong, Monica S., and Paul Gillian. 1992. "The Changing Role of Women in Employment in Eastern Europe." Report 8213. Washington, D.C.: World Bank.

Gill, I., G. Sedlacek, and R. Nayar. 1993. Forthcoming. "Gender and Employment: Implications of Household Responsibilities for Access and Rewards to Market Work." In A.V. Adams, L. Riveros, and E.M. King, eds., *Managing the Social Cost of Adjustment*. Washington, D.C.: World Bank.

Godinho, Joana 1994. "Reproductive Health during the Economic Transition in Belarus, Estonia, Georgia, and Uzbekistan." World Bank, Europe and Central Asia Country Department, Washington, D.C.

Harriss, Barbara, S. Guhan, and R. H. Cassen, eds. 1992. *Poverty in India: Research and Policy*. Bombay: Oxford University Press.

Herz Barbara, and S. Khandker. 1991. *Women's Work, Education, and Family Welfare in Peru*. World Bank Discussion Paper 116. Washington, D.C.

Herz, Barbara, K. Subbarao, Masooma Habib, and Laura Raney. 1991. *Letting Girls Learn: Promising Approaches in Primary and Secondary Education*. World Bank Discussion Paper 133. Washington, D.C.

Holt, Sharon, and Helena Ribe. 1991. *Developing Financial Institutions for the Poor and Reducing Barriers to Access for Women*. World Bank Discussion Paper 117. Washington, D.C.

International Labor Office. Various years. *Yearbook of Statistics*. Geneva, Switzerland.

International Food Policy Research Institute. 1992. *Understanding How Resources Are Allocated Within Households*. Washington, D.C.

Jamison, Dean, and M. Lockheed. 1987. "Participation in Schooling: Determinants and Learning Outcomes in Nepal." *Economic Development and Cultural Change* 35(2):279–306.

Jimenez, E., and M. Lockheed. 1989. "Enhancing Girls' Learning through Single-Sex Education: Evidence and a Policy Conundrum." *Educational Evaluation and Policy Analysis* 11:117–42.

Katz, E. 1993. "Women's Health and Nutrition." World Bank, Education and Social Policy Department, Washington, D.C.

Khandker, S. 1993. "Schooling Outcomes and School Efficiency in Bangladesh." World Bank, Education and Social Policy Department, Washington, D.C.

Khandker, S., and V. Levy. 1993. "Schooling and Cognitive Achievements of Children in Morocco: Can the Government Improve Outcomes?" World Bank, Education and Social Policy Department, Washington, D.C.

King, Elizabeth, and Lee A. Lillard. 1987. "Education Policy and Schooling Attainment in Malaysia and the Philippines." *Economics of Education Review* 6:167–81.

King, Elizabeth, and M.A. Hill, eds. 1993. *Women's Education in Developing Countries: Barriers, Benefits, and Policies*. Baltimore, Md.: Johns Hopkins University Press.

Lee, Valerie E., and Marlaine E. Lockheed. 1990. "The Effects of Single-Sex Schooling on Student Achievement and Attitudes in Nigeria." *Comparative Education Review* 34(2):209–32.

Le Vine, Robert A. 1982. "Influences of Women's Schooling on Maternal Behavior in the Third World." In Gail Kelly and C. Elliott, eds., *Women's Education in the Third World*. Albany, N.Y.: State University of New York Press.

Mehra, R., D. Bruns, P. Carlson, G. R. Gupta, and M. Lycette. 1992. *Engendering Development in Asia and the Near East: A Sourcebook.* Washington, D.C.: International Center for Research on Women.

Moghadam, V.M., ed. 1993. *Democratic Reform and the Position of Women in Transitional Economies.* Oxford, U.K.: Clarendon Press.

Moghadam, V.M. 1990a. "Gender and Restructuring: Perestroika, the 1989 Revolution, and Women." WIDER Working Paper 87. Helsinki.

———. 1990b. "Determinants of Female Labor Force Participation in the Middle East and North Africa." WIDER Working Paper 85. Helsinki.

Moock, Peter. 1976. "The Efficiency of Women as Farm Managers: Kenya." *American Journal of Agricultural Economics* 58(5):831–35.

Moser, Caroline O. N. 1989. "Gender Planning in the Third World: Meeting Practical and Strategic Gender Needs." *World Development* 17(November):1799–825.

———. 1993. *Gender Planning and Development: Theory, Practice and Training.* London: Routledge.

Over, Mead. 1992. "The Macroeconomic Impact of AIDS in Sub-Saharan Africa." World Bank, Africa Technical Department. Washington, D.C.

Psacharopoulos, G., and Z. Tzannatos. 1992. *Women's Employment and Pay in Latin America: Overview and Methodology.* Washington, D.C.: World Bank.

Quisumbing, A. 1993. "Women in Agriculture." World Bank, Education and Social Policy Department, Washington, D.C.

Rhyne, E., and S. Holt. 1993. "Women in Finance and Enterprise Development." World Bank, Education and Social Policy Department, Washington, D.C.

Saito, Katrine Anderson, Hailu Mekonnen, and Daphne Spurling. 1992. "Raising the Productivity of Women Farmers in Sub-Saharan Africa." World Bank Discussion Paper 230. Washington, D.C.

Schultz, T. P. 1993. "Returns to Women's Education." In Elizabeth King and Ann Hill, eds., *Women's Education in Developing Countries: Barriers, Benefits, and Policies.* Baltimore, Md.: Johns Hopkins University Press.

Sedlacek, Guilherme. 1993. "The Role of Labor Markets in the Colombian Poverty Assessment." World Bank, Education and Social Policy Department, Washington, D.C.

Sedlacek, Guilherme, and D. Lam. 1993. "Women's Education, Female Labor Supply and Fertility Decline in Brazil." World Bank, Education and Social Policy Department, Washington, D.C.

Sedlacek, Guilherme, L. Gutierrez, and A. Mohindra. 1993. "Women in the Labor Market." World Bank, Education and Social Policy Department, Washington, D.C.

Searle, B. 1989. Personal communication to the authors of "Letting Girls Learn."

Simpson-Hebert, Mayling. 1984. "Water and Sanitation: Cultural Considerations." In Peter G. Bourne, ed., *Water and Sanitation: Economic and Sociological Perspectives.* New York: Academic Press.

Singh, R.D., and M.J. Morey. 1987. "The Value of Work-at-Home and Contributions of Wives' Household Service in Polygamous Families: Evidence from an African LDC." *Economic Development and Cultural Change* 35:743–65.

Subbarao, K. 1993. "Interventions to Fill Nutrition Gaps at the Household Level: A Review of India's Experience." In B. Harris and Robert Cassen, eds., *Poverty: Research and Policy in India.* New Delhi: Oxford University Press.

Subbarao, K., and L. Raney. 1993. *Social Gains from Female Education: A Cross-National Study.*" World Bank Discussion Paper 194. Washington, D.C.

Summers, Lawrence. 1992. "Investing in All the People: Educating Women in Developing Countries." EDI Seminar Paper 45. Washington, D.C.: World Bank.

Tinker, Anne G., and Joana Godinho. 1994. "Investments in Women's Health in Central and Eastern European Countries." World Bank, Europe and Central Asia Country Department, Washington, D.C.

Tinker, Anne G., Marjorie A. Koblinsky, and Patricia Daly. 1993. *Making Motherhood Safe.* World Bank Discussion Paper 202. Washington, D.C.

United Nations. 1991. *The World's Women: Trends and Statistics, 1970–90.* New York.

———. 1992. *The Impact of Economic and Political Reform on the Status of Women in Eastern Europe: Proceedings of a United Nations Regional Seminar.* New York.

United Nations Statistical Office. 1990. *United Nations Women's Indicators and Statistics Spreadsheet Database for Microcomputers, WISTAT, Version 2.* New York.

———. 1991. *The World's Women, 1970–1990: Trends and Statistics.* New York.

WHO. 1992. "Uzbekistan: Country Highlights." Copenhagen: World Health Organization, Europe.

Wijaya, Hesti R. 1985. "Women's Access to Land Resources: Some Observations from East Javanese Rural Agriculture." In The International Rice Research Institute, *Women in Rice Farming: Proceedings of a Conference on Women in Rice-Farming Systems.* Brookfield, U.K.: Gower.

World Bank. 1992. *World Development Report 1992.* New York: Oxford University Press.

———. 1993a. *World Development Report 1993.* New York: Oxford University Press.

———. 1993b. "Uganda: Growing out of Poverty." Country Economic Memorandum. Washington, D.C.

World Bank, Education and Social Policy Department. 1993c. "Progress Report on the World Bank's Activities on Women in Development." Washington, D.C.

World Bank, Population Health and Nutrition Department. Draft. "Women's Health and Nutrition: Making a Difference." Washington, D.C.